Out of Our Lives II

ELIZABETH LÉONIE SIMPSON

iUniverse, Inc.
New York Bloomington

iUniverse books may be ordered through booksellers or by contacting:

iUniverse
1663 Liberty Drive
Bloomington, IN 47403
www.iuniverse.com
1-800-Authors (1-800-288-4677)

Because of the dynamic nature of the Internet, any Web addresses or links contained in this book may have changed since publication and may no longer be valid. The views expressed in this work are solely those of the author and do not necessarily reflect the views of the publisher, and the publisher hereby disclaims any responsibility for them.

ISBN: 978-1-4401-4745-6 (sc)
ISBN: 978-1-4401-4746-3 (ebook)

Printed in the United States of America

iUniverse rev. date: 6/29/2009

This book, the second written by retired residents living in this community, is dedicated to them and their willingness to share their lives with others. Linda Blodgett and William Ferguson, who designed and furnished the photograph for the cover, made many useful suggestions.

In remembering, we come to things of importance. That arrival, however, is not effected without shifts and swirls, along a poorly illuminated, sometimes difficult, passage. And at the end of its dim tortuousness what we find at our destination are products of our own making, constructions we have made of value that matter to us.

TABLE OF CONTENTS

PREFACE

"Don't try it. You'll only make enemies in a village where you expect to live out the rest of your life." That was what I was told when I began testing the idea of putting together a book by us and about us, the members of our community. [1] Being an independent soul, I forewarned any likely participants that I would fully implement my rights as editor. That didn't deter them. Fellow residents started writing. For me, the result was many months of pleasurable hard work, pleasure largely derived from the opportunity to get to know them in ways that otherwise, even with luck, might have taken years of casual encounter or careful planning.

Everyone has to live with stereotypes during some part of his or her life and elders are no exception. Certainly we, in our particular retirement community, are not all stamped out of the same metal, dull and repetitious, with no shining individual sparks. Not at all! The years may not have added physical grace or intellectual wisdom to every one of us, but they certainly have provided diversity of experience--the kind of diversity and knowledge that would not be found in 18-year-olds however charming and bright. The telling of these tales feeds curiosity about others and satisfies it royally.

We may go into the unknown as we age, but there is no hollow blank left behind us. Instead, we leave full paths extending outward, crowded with memory in our thinking selves. We may live in that center, without knowledge of remote beginning or of inevitable end, but like the bird, the flower, or the raindrop, we are not alone.

---

[1] Saratoga Retirement Community, Saratoga, California, a facility owned and operated by the Odd Fellows and Rebekahs of California

What I wanted for this book (and its predecessor) was a vital expression of the reality of the person writing, a being both individual and together with others. Most of us share the impulse to reach out, to extract what others have learned from experience. No one wants to hear everything and, fortunately, no one tries to tell everything. The choice of what to leave out is always the prerogative of the writer, but a book in any form, large or small, is still an act of reaching out for connection.

Some of us were already in the process of writing up our life stories for our descendants or in hope of publication for a wider readership. A few had finished that task and among them were several willing to share a portion of what they had written. Sometimes that was useful, but not always. Sometimes, as collector and editor, I have experienced an unexpected shock of anxiety. How could I tactfully suggest that the manuscripts I was given were not suitable for our book? That happened several times.

A few years before his arrival at the Saratoga Retirement Community, for example, one of our residents had been asked by his mid-western university to write about his educational experience there for a 50th reunion publication. Unknown to me, he gave me what he had written as his contribution to our proposed volume. It contained lengthy detailed descriptions of his courses and the professors who taught them. Included there, too, were a few provocative lines about his upbringing during the Great Depression, his service during the Second World War, and his marriage. The *person* I was after (and who I thought our readership would be interested in) was missing from the essay. Not being fellow students at that time and place, our readers would not be emotionally involved by the tale he was telling, the experience he was describing. In fact, they would probably be bored, flip over the pages, or close the book.

Steadying myself for his possible withdrawal from our project, when I sat down with him I told him that I thought he had two good choices for a proper contribution, that is, an essay that would interest a wide variety of readers. Those two were, first, the Depression years of his youth or, second, his war service. He shook his head and went away without saying a word. I thought that was that: he was giving up. But later he called me. In his files he had found a description of those earlier family years that he had put together for a granddaughter, and he offered it to me as his substitute submission. I read it, and we were both pleased. It turned out to be just the sort of personal account I was after--a meaningful one for a readership extending beyond his family doors.

There were many nights when exploratory conversation flowed across our dinner tables during pauses in service. Some stories told during those mealtimes were too personal or too painful to be recorded and shared in print. They were refused because the memories they tapped were too private and, if the tellers decided to discuss them at all, it would only be with their own descendents.

There were also residents who wouldn't consider having their stories written and shared because they thought their lives had been so ordinary that no one would be interested.

A former ballet dancer told of her professional life and contacts with great dancers; a nurse recounted her work with Latin American nurses. An experienced bird watcher talked about those distinctive flyers she had seen around the world and helped us residents identify our local birds. Rumors of an accidental fire set by a resident and even of bars of precious gold wrapped in a blanket and hidden in an apartment bathroom were circulated. A retired doctor told how her mother had disappeared from home for two weeks to force her son to abandon his Protestant fiancée in favor of a woman with the mother's religious beliefs. Interesting as they were, none of these tales was offered for this book.

One evening a narrative spun out vividly across the dining room table was that of a Jewish family during Hitler's regime in Nazi Germany. The teller believed it was too common a tale to be interesting to readers and, anyway, he thought it might trouble the other German residents with whom we share our daily community activities. Like many others, that mealtime disclosure didn't make it into our book.

Day after day, I never felt that I had to poke or prod to get either slight or lengthy verbal contributions from my fellow diners!

For others of our German residents who had lived through the Second World War the past had been ceaselessly haunting. One woman insisted that there were many who jeopardized their own lives by hiding Jews. She remembered the post-war Russian occupation of East Germany, where her family lived, as far more traumatic than the years under Hitler. Another German, defensively, described her inability to talk about those times. The dictator had been believed when he said he would bring the country back to greatness, but he disappointed his people as disastrous events rolled on and on.

Sober-faced and looking away from those of us listening, a veteran of the Second World War recounted the day the damaged seaplane he was piloting crashed on land with what he called the miracle of only one occupant being killed. In a different wartime episode, one of his friends had been shot down over a Pacific island occupied by the Japanese. As the survivors fled the wrecked plane, they were caught one by one and beheaded. That retiree could tell us about these dire happenings over a convivial dinner, but he couldn't bear to have them written in detail for publication. Almost sixty years later these events were still too disturbing to share with a wider public.

Another evening a lovely ninety-two-year-old, by then living with a bridge-playing ninety-five-year-old widower, described a past turning point in her life. That was the night when her first husband walked out the door, as he usually did, to buy an evening paper and was robbed and killed on a San Francisco street. She turned from a coddled, dependent woman into a successful business entrepreneur, assuming her dead husband's role in the larger world.

Every resident's story was different from the others.

When a young woman was marrying an Italian professor, her Chinese mother, a nuclear physicist, made her first attempt at sewing clothing. She wanted to make her daughter's wedding dress and she, who was so successful in solving what she considered to be much more difficult problems, found herself beset with novel ones. The outcome was a frustrating, comic series of trials ending with all the seams of the formal dress held together with invisible masking tape. The story of her trials was given to me in convoluted basic English. In my role as editor, I re-wrote the chapter for future presentation, maintaining the writer's style and the point of the finally successful endeavor, but putting it into more standard language. My revision was completely acceptable to her, but when the physicist showed the article to her daughter, the young woman told her mother that she didn't know that she could write so well! Neither one of us told her the truth.

More life stories were yet to come.

A train stalled for a week in a Wyoming snow storm, six months on Oahu with little parental restraint when the writer was twelve years old , a hurricane in the Bahamas, fantasies about a beloved dress, and the recovery of lost self-confidence one night in Paris--these formed some of the wild pullings from the backgrounds of varied experience. A Department of Motor Vehicles tester learned what a difference one word can make when she mistakenly instructed her applicant driver to turn *"izquierdo"* instead of *"derecho"*, substituting *"left"* for *"right"* in Spanish. Another contributor wrote about the pleasure of participating in a closed community of scientists working on the atomic bomb Manhattan Project.

As I wrote earlier, I wasn't always entirely content with the material offered me. A possible contributor refused to produce a second entry after I told him that I thought the first one about missing the train home from a dance in London was amusing, but too trivial to fit with the others being offered. What I wanted from him was an essay imbued with the culture and the values of the time he had lived in a particular social class. I knew that he had a very different background from the rest of us average middle-class Americans. I wanted him to share how his experience in the Army had shaken him out of the cocoon of that wealthy British existence--one his mother referred to gently as "comfortable." In the end he gave me just what I wanted: a detailed chapter from what he is planning to be memoirs for his own children.

I discovered early in my residence at SRC that one great advantage of connections made within such a community is the variation of patterns in our long lives. As many others have said, diversity is the spice of life. There are no clones here and no duplicate action settings from which any two of us came. To begin with, in the book we have already made together, *Out of Our Lives,* our histories originated in twelve countries (Canada, the United Kingdom, Germany, China, Japan, France, Spain, Uganda, Turkey, New Guinea, the Solomon Islands, and seven of our United States.). Complementing that range of beginnings were the numerous professions and enterprises the writers had chosen over the course of their lifetimes. There was at least one of each of the following: medical doctor, art therapist, weaver and spinner, paleontologist, photographer, psychologist, as well as a number of physicists, artists, and sculptors. Some of us have been honored in the course of our lives. Others have famous antecedents or can be called up on the Internet for a variety of other reasons. We have met each other only by fortunate accident and what we have produced together in that earlier book was separate slices of real life, joined by our overlapping time spans.

In this second volume neither the origins nor the occupations of the writers are as widespread and diverse as in the previous one. However, the range of experience is equally great, from misery to joy, expressed in the words of the human actors.

Such remembrance bolsters us, lifts us, feeds us into knowing who we really are. By sharing these portions of our lives with others, we can never again be entirely apart. That which is expressed, enacted, said, or written, counts for much in this entangling world. From time to time, to our great benefit, a willful silence spills into growth, person to person, into passages of connection. What would be sadder than humanity without these means of connection? In one of his poems the Jesuit priest, Gerard Manley Hopkins, asked God to send his roots rain, to bring his self into full being the way that seedlings are nourished into maturity and fulfillment. For those who wrote the pages appearing in this book, these necessary drops have already fallen and the potential crop of completeness has sprouted.

Out of each of our lives has come marrow bone memory. Here in this community, and this book, is experience ingested into mutuality. And though we continue in this new volume with different participants, some who wrote for the first book and have more that they want to pour out, to claim as their own and share, now wait for a future opportunity. With both today's and tomorrow's writers, our explorations of the past continue. The search is vital for us, one that is renewing, expansive, and supportive within our everyday present.

Elizabeth Léonie Simpson, Editor

WILLIE SUTTON AND ME

Malcolm E. "Buck" Sample

In 1952 the famous many-time bank robber, Willie Sutton, was captured in the streets of New York City by Police Department Detective Donald Shea on the Joint Bank Robbery Task Force. He had been spotted in a subway by an 18-year-old Brooklynite named Arnold Schuster. Already famous, it was at least partly because, when he was asked why he robbed banks, Sutton replied, "That's where the money is!" Arnold had followed him because he knew that there was an $100,000 reward for the person who furnished information that would lead to his capture. A new patrolman, Shea was loading beer into his marked police car to take it to his son's baptism party when Schuster came up to him. Donald Shea didn't believe him and didn't want to get involved, but the citizen reporting to him was so insistent that he finally arrested the robber. When Schuster went to the police station demanding the reward for turning the man in to the police, his request was refused and patrolman Shea himself was pushed aside by senior officers.

When he hired an attorney and returned to try to claim the announced reward, Arnold produced threatening anonymous letters he had received—letters that warned him that Sutton's friends would be after him. Although the Police Captain read the letters, he chose to ignore them. Schuster and his attorney got nowhere that day, but soon afterwards went to the FBI to try again.

That's where I came in.

I listened to his story and put all the information on record. Later that Friday afternoon another Special Agent and I went to Brooklyn to take Arnold Schuster's and his father's fingerprints for elimination purposes. At that time the letters had been handled by both son and father, their attorney, and the police Captain so there was no way to prove that the Captain had handled the papers before they were sent.

The next day, Saturday, Arnold was walking down the street when he was murdered gangland-style from a passing car. (Many years later information came out that he was killed by one of Sutton's associates to discourage people from cooperating with law enforcement.)

The FBI and the Department of Justice took the position that the murder was a local matter and should be investigated by the New York City Police Department. The NYC Commissioner of Police said that this was a Willie Sutton bank robbery matter and was solely under the jurisdiction of the federal government. Bobby Kennedy, the United States Attorney General, disagreed. Acrimonious correspondence ensued. Eventually Schuster's parents sued the city of New York for a million dollars for not protecting their son. However, prior to Schuster's death, his father had told the other agent and me that he had refused that protection because he didn't think it was needed. The District Attorney for the County of New York subpoenaed me and the other Special Agent to testify at the trial. Attorney General Kennedy ordered us to answer the subpoena but respectfully decline to testify. If we didn't, we would have been in contempt of court and the city would not have had the benefit of that testimony to support its case. So, after numerous telephone conversations between the DA and the Attorney General, we testified anyway.

That testimony was a deciding factor in the outcome of the trial. The jury found for the city and no damages were awarded.

Willie Sutton spent the rest of his life in prison, but the Schusters got no reward for their son's recognizing and turning in the bank robber.

But there is a funny part of the story which was told to me by a fellow officer who is still in touch with retired Donald Shea. At the time, the Police Commissioner thought that the patrolman should have been rewarded by promotion for turning in Sutton. Thinking this was the rank where a detective would start, he made him a first-grade one. Everyone around him was afraid to tell the Commissioner that this was the highest grade a detective could ever earn. He should have started at the bottom with grade three.

COPING

Deanna Viale

On September 29th of 1952 on a beautiful, late summer day I was transferring from one class to another in my first year at junior high school. It was a sprawling school, and I was heading from one large building to another. As I ran down the stairs, I noticed that my head was pounding with a terrible headache and my eyes seemed to have difficulty focusing. Instead of opening the glass door, I crashed right into it, fell backward, and hit my head on the cement flooring. I was carried to the nurse's office and my mother was called. I had a large welt on the back of my head, as well as one on my forehead, but I was most concerned about missing my 6th period class. What was this class, you ask? Girl's PE. Something I loved.

I was taken home to bed with a significant fever, and the family physician, a dear friend, was called. He came to the house immediately. By then my father was home from work and soon I heard my parents whispering with him outside my door that I was going to the hospital. My parents explained to me that I needed some tests done to evaluate how sick I was. My father carried me down the stairs; I remember that my favorite television program, *Life With Luigi*, was playing.

At the hospital I was given a spinal tap and my parents were told that I had polio, not spinal meningitis. This diagnosis was not shared with me until some time later. I was then placed in the isolation ward, told to remain in bed and not to move. My parents were not permitted to come in. They stood outside the door with protective masks on, waving at me, trying to comfort me from that distance. Of course, I was extremely

16

frightened. I must have rung the buzzer to ask for a bed pan because one was handed to me. But I didn't know how to use it. When the nurse disappeared, I set it on the table beside me, got up, and used the bathroom to the right of my bed. As I was returning, I fell and when the nurse returned to retrieve the bed pan, I was lying on the floor, bewildered, still unable to get up. She was annoyed that I hadn't followed her instructions, but she called the orderly anyway to put me back into my bed.

For the next day or two my breathing was constantly being evaluated through a device placed over my mouth. During all of this I was so feverish that I was fading in and out of consciousness. As they rolled a giant "can" into my room, they told me that this machine would increase my breathing capacity and make me more comfortable. I was scared by it, but that frightening lung became my home for the next two months, the first two weeks of which were still in isolation. The whole thing was unimaginable. My head stuck out the top while the remainder of my body was left within. Try scratching your nose under those conditions!

The elderly nurse attending me was no help. I had to ask for anything I wanted in a specific way. If she didn't like how I said what I needed, she didn't do it. She would ignore me. Since I didn't want the hospital food, she ate what was provided me—especially if it were lamb chops. I didn't know then that I was in an infectious unit, but later, when I found out, I wondered why she thought it was safe to eat my food. She wore only a mask and white gown, but no protective gloves. She must have known the danger because she was obviously afraid to touch me. (At my request my parents brought me milk shakes which were much easier to eat than lamb chops.)

After this isolation period, still in the iron lung, I was moved into a ward with other children, some also in lungs and others in beds. The nursing staff was better trained and much more receptive to working with children. My parents could come to visit me there twice a day. My mother came in every afternoon, bringing my little brother and my Nona (grandmother). My ward was on the second floor, but the two of them stayed down below in an open area where he rode his tricycle. I could watch them out the window through the mirror attached to my iron lung. It was the highlight of my day! Normalcy, joy, and family!

While I was in the iron lung, I was treated with Sister Kenny hot packs. These wool pieces of fabric were steam-heated, wrapped around the limb, and covered with plastic for heat retention. When I returned home, my mother did this for me twice a day. I'll never forget the smell of that wet wool or the warmth of her devotion!

During the first week of November the medical staff began weaning me from the iron lung with short stays outside. I was lifted out and placed in a bed for periods of 15 minutes, then up to half an hour, and later a full hour several times a day. My doctors didn't believe that I needed any oxygen support system and this long process of getting to breathe for myself was very frightening to me.

My parents, knowing that my recovery would be enhanced by family environment, volunteered to follow the therapeutic regime prescribed by the physicians and made me up a hospital bed in the living room at home. My return on Thanksgiving Day was my first ride in an ambulance. I, still lying down, entered our front door, encountering the strong fragrance of the cooking turkey. My reaction? I proceeded to vomit all over my clean clothes. (This was not the reason I later became a vegetarian.)

Physical and occupational therapists, doing exercises with me and instructing both of my parents, came to see me twice a week. Getting to a seated position and eventually to a chair was a long and arduous process. My first wheelchair was a hard wooden one with a tall, straight back of woven cane. It had large wheels and a bedpan insertion stored under the seat. Just what a young person wants her friends to see! In the beginning, those friends were very faithful and extremely welcome but, as time went by, they increasingly went back to their usual lives and those visits diminished. Not having the support of modern technology, I felt increasingly isolated.

My solution? I became a member of the Kensington Library. With the librarian's willing assistance, my parents brought appropriate books home for me. I read everything I was given, including volumes of the Nancy Drew series, Louisa M. Alcott's *Little Women*, E. B. White's *Stuart Little*, and A. A. Milne's *Winnie the Pooh*. For a long time I lived vicariously through these fascinating characters.

As my physical abilities increased, I set myself a goal of being able to return to my own room on the second floor by the first of the year. I could stand with my long leg braces, but I couldn't walk. I could, however, flop off the wheelchair, and scoot myself across the floor backwards, propelled by my arms. I practiced on the lowest steps, using those arms to lift myself over and over again. Gradually I could ascend more than one step at a time and, on New Year's Eve, I reached my goal: I successfully negotiated all 18 steps.

Perhaps my ability to do this, and to make the other tough choices that came along, originated in my father's steadfast character and my closeness to him. He would never allow me to say "No! I can't!" but instead would assist me in solving the problems

I faced. "There is always a way!" It wasn't an oral motto, but it was strongly implied and I understood his meaning. His strength of mind showed clearly when he insisted that, when I returned to public schooling, I was to go to the usual kind, one designed for a great cross-section of children. In short, I should return to the school where I had been before I became ill, not one for the permanently physically challenged.

Before I did go back to that junior high school I had two years of home schooling with a warm, gifted, caring teacher coming three days a week. She always came in a clean white wool blazer with her hair tied up in a knot on the top of her head. Accessible and encouraging, she made keeping up with my absent classmates fun, as well as challenging. I learned French from her with such a good accent that it carried over to my return to public school.

Every day my mother drove me to and from my ninth grade classes at Portola Junior High. Once there, the matron assisted me to and from the restroom and from class to class when the distance was too great for me to manage alone. Later the three-story high school was another building, in another place. It had no elevator, but I could pull myself up by holding on to the banister and turning sideways. Mom pulled the wheelchair up those stairs all the way to my first period class. After that, the custodian moved me from class to class. When I was about 14, after school I began volunteering at Herrick Hospital as a Candy Striper. It was basically paper work, but still satisfying. At the end of my time there I was honored as the young Candy Striper with the most hours volunteered.

When I turned 16, I earned my driver's license and, using the hand control, could maneuver our family car. Getting to El Cerrito High School and back again was no problem. I picked up my friends on the way and, once there, they helped me out of the car and into my wheelchair. At the end of the day we did the reverse. Many of this loyal group of friends went on to the University of California at Berkeley along with me and have continued to be livelong friends.

The two summers before I graduated from high school I had two operations to stabilize my ankles so I could walk without using the long-leg braces. During my senior year I spent several hours after school at the company where my father worked, learning to teletype, do transcription, and PBX--the elaborate telephone system. This went on to serve me well in providing tuition money for college.

For me, the terrain at Berkeley was really challenging. My high school friends were my support system, along with some of the university's service fraternities. When I and one other similar student arrived, there was no provision for those who were wheelchair bound, so the help of these boys was very much needed. Because of my love for children, I majored in child development. But after graduation when I applied to work for my teaching credential, I soon found out that the School of Education would not admit me since my practice teaching would have to be in that hilly environment. That was one that, to them, looked impossibly difficult for me in a wheelchair.

So I applied to San José State which was willing to accept me but would not guarantee my success at finding a position--a guarantee they gave routinely to the graduates from their program. However, with the encouragement of my two resident supervisors, I completed the course of study and was awarded a position in the local school district. The times they were a-changing!

There I spent some 34 years, teaching first and second graders and being taught by them. I began teaching in January of 1968 when it rained solidly for the first two weeks. Within just a few days I had exhausted all my rainy day materials and begun to wonder about this chosen career. Fortunately, my more seasoned colleagues encouraged me and shared their material.

For a beginning teacher, maintaining discipline among some 30-plus children can be quite a challenge. Seeing me in a wheelchair, they simply assumed that they had an advantage. However, when they were noisy, I soon learned an effective way of quieting them: I wheeled myself over to a child who was particularly loud, placed my hands on his desk, and pulled myself up to a standing position. The reaction was total silence in the classroom.

I had one shy little boy who wouldn't take home his work for those first two weeks. His parents called to ask if the school policy about weekly work had changed. Although I had taken such pride in creating this work and writing personal comments to each student, he had left his behind. He wasn't going to do it. I was an interloper. He had been fond of his previous teacher and he wanted no part of me. I wasn't his *real* teacher and, besides, I was right out of college. Once I had interacted with his parents, things changed. At the end of the school year they wrote me that their son was often scooting around the family room in his rocking chair, being the teacher in the wheelchair and teaching his little sister. Needless to say, that pleased me.

Being a twin is not an easy situation. Over the years in which I taught I had several sets of twins. Some parents wish to have their twins separated; others prefer them to be in the same classroom. One year there was the cutest little freckled-faced, brown-haired, blue-eyed boy who had a twin sister in another classroom. Of course, this was the first year for them to be separated since they had been together in kindergarten. To this day I remember exactly where he sat in my classroom. Checking with each student after teaching a lesson as I always did, I went by his desk and found him trying to mask his tears, blinking very quickly. He was missing his twin sister. As I approached, I winked at him. Really surprised, for just a second he closed both eyes, trying to wink back. At the early fall conference his mother and I were discussing his progress when she mentioned that her son thought I wasn't giving him any help. All I did was wink at him! By the second conference in late January, he no longer was teary-eyed and, besides, had actually learned how to wink back.

I was teaching when the Pillsbury dough boy was introduced in advertising. He was made of dough and when he was gently poked, it would leave an indentation and he would giggle. During the first years of early education children are encouraged to be seated on the floor at the foot of the teacher while she is reading a story. One very hot day while I was reading one to them, I felt a little girl very gently rubbing the instep of my foot. My feet were quite swollen and the swelling extended out over the sides of my shoes. I continued reading aloud. She pressed her finger into my instep and exclaimed, "Oh, Miss Viale! You're just like the Pillsbury dough boy! You're puffing out all over!" Both I and the other children laughed, but I couldn't help thinking that this bright girl was using some high level thinking skills when she made a remark like that.

For the first 25 years of my career my hair was long and I wore it in a chignon, tucked at the back of my head. Due to physical changes, it became necessary for me to cut my hair very short. When I returned to school in September to set up my classroom, one of my former students was circling the quad on his bike. The first time around he hesitated, but he didn't stop. The second time around he stopped and asked, "Miss Viale, is that you?" Of course I replied that it was. He kept looking at my hair and, to my delight, called out, "Wow! You look so much younger!" before he wheeled off.

As the Americans with Disability Act of the early 90s began to be enforced, the presence of the physically challenged became more evident. In the 1992 Nordstrom spring catalog there was a young boy on crutches featured as one of the models. I decided to try my hand at this, too. I sent off a series of photographs, some from my classroom, with a letter introducing myself to the Nordstrom advertising department. It was a crazy idea, but I wanted to try. To my great surprise I received an offer to fly to Seattle for the Christmas catalog shoot. Then, for the next two years, I was featured in both the Christmas and spring catalogs. I autographed these for my students who couldn't believe those photographs were of their teacher.

I'm still in touch with many of my former students. One of these is a dark-eyed girl with a wonderful smile. Early in her first-grade year she told me that she wanted to grow up to be a teacher just like me because I always smelled so good. We kept in touch over the years. After four years of college she re-appeared and told me that she had finally learned what my perfume was: Este Lauder's Youth Dew! She was wearing it herself. The most thrilling part of that visit was her announcement that she had achieved her credential and had an assignment as a first-grade teacher.

A teacher's dream is to have students who choose to make teaching their careers. These of mine and others, including a little boy, have greatly rewarded me by undertaking this profession. And, to my great pleasure, they have told me that their memories of my classes were the source of their later career choices.

MY FIRST MISSION:

Bombing During World War II

Alan Purchase

PROLOG

I volunteered for the Army Air Corps at age 17 and was called to duty in July of 1943, two months after turning 18. We were immediately loaded onto a troop train headed for Texas. The first stop was Shepherd Field, Wichita Falls in north Texas for six weeks of basic training. Putting it mildly, growing up in an upper middle-class neighborhood in Oakland, California did not prepare me for the shock of Army life. The first night at Shepherd Field was spent under a canvas tarp with a dozen other recruits, trying to sleep on the ground with only one blanket serving as mattress and cover. The next day we were issued uniforms and immediately threw away the clothes we had worn for the last six days. They were filthy from the dirt, dust, and soot accumulated during five days of stop-and-go troop travel, sleeping two in the lower bunk, one the upper, and no showers.

Our barracks were badly over-crowded. At night we often resorted to dragging our mattresses down from the second story to sleep on a patch of lawn, even though we had to be up, dressed, looking spick-and-span with beds made military fashion by four in the morning. That was when we lined up into platoons and marched briskly to the mess hall for breakfast. It was not exactly the routine I was used to, not at all like life at home!

My next stop was Henderson State Teachers College in Arkadelphia, Arkansas, for academic study not as advanced as I had in high school. Arkadelphia was a small town with one drug store, two gas stations, and three large churches, with blacks living in squalor on its edge. I was a cadet officer and quickly learned that, if I walked like I knew where I was going and carried a clipboard, no one ever questioned me.

Next came Ellington Field, Houston, for aviation cadet training, then Lorado on the southern border of Texas for gunnery school. That was fun for everyone except the poor pilots who were pulling the airborne targets. Several had been shot down by mistake. I even stood up in an open cockpit plane, shooting at both airborne and ground targets. We also became very proficient at skeet shooting, using shotguns to shoot at clay disks that mechanical triggers fired out in various directions. That was an enjoyable skill I would never again use.

Then came testing and classification at Lincoln, Nebraska. I had my choice of pilot, navigator, or bombardier training, but knew, if I chose pilot, at six feet I was too tall for fighters and, as a 19-year-old, I would only be a co-pilot. I didn't want to be a bombardier and, since I liked math, navigator was a natural choice. I was assigned to navigation school at San Marcos, in the middle of Texas.

After 14 months of service, in August of 1944, I was commissioned a second lieutenant and received my navigator's wings. Following graduation I was assigned to a new flight crew at Biggs Army Air Force Base, El Paso, to train on B-17 "Flying Fortress" bombers. I'm sure some powers that be had looked at my record and decided that, since I had already been stationed in the north, south, east, and central parts of Texas, I should experience west Texas.

Being assigned to this crew was my good fortune. Our pilot was 27, several years older than average, with considerable flying experience. He had grown up in Alaska where he was a part-time bush pilot. He had also been an instructor pilot on B-17s so he knew our airplane very well.

REMEMBRANCES

The temperature hitting a record 112 degrees at Wichita Falls while we were jogging on dusty roads, in heavy GI boots, out at Shepherd Field. I lost 14 pounds in less than six weeks.

Learning to drink beer while stationed at Lorado. The water was not drinkable due to color, aroma, visible impurities, and taste. It took me four sessions before I could finish one bottle, but then I got the hang of it.

Doing guard duty at night in freezing rain at Ellington Field, patrolling outside our barracks with a wooden rifle. Welcome to Army life!

Seeing a shanty town where blacks lived on the outskirts of Arkadelphia, Arkansas. Discrimination was foreign to me, growing up in a nice district of Oakland, California in the 1930s and '40s.

While stationed at San Marcos, watching thunderheads form, growing from small, pretty, white clouds in the late morning to awesome, full-fledged menaces by evening.

Getting my first three-day pass in nine months and going into San Antonio. After four hours of wandering around, I returned to our base to play gin rummy with friends.

Flying over west Texas and New Mexico at night, sitting in the Plexiglas nose of a B-17. I saw spectacular skies, often filled with shooting stars. They were awe-inspiring.

B-24s had been stationed at Biggs Field prior to our arrival. After several crashed into the Franklin Mountains that rose up off the end of the runway, they were exchanged for B-17s. Every time we took off, as our plane struggled to gain enough altitude to clear the mountains, we could see black scars directly in front of us.

TRANSITION TO EUROPE

Upon completion of our training came assignment to the 8th Air Force based in England and so, in December, we crossed the North Atlantic on the French liner *Normandy*, traveling at full speed and without any escort. Our choice had been either to try to outrun submarines or to stay in a slow-moving convoy. Life on board was not pleasant for officers, worse for the enlisted men who slept in five-high canvas bunks. The stench from sea sickness was pervasive.

Arriving in Scotland we talked with some of the locals and quickly realized we could not understand a word they were saying. Awaiting orders, we slept on thin straw mattresses on wooden platforms in a very cold monastery.

Our crew was assigned to the 384th Bomb Group, 546th Squadron, stationed at Grafton Underwood, a "two-pub" village in the Midlands where our base was affectionately referred to as "Grafton Undermud."

I had to learn to drink beer all over again. The English pub beer was warm, weak and bitter, but I got the hang of it quickly. I also had to learn to drink scotch since bourbon was in very short supply. The base regularly sent planes to Scotland on "training missions." (I still have my taste for scotch and couldn't care less for bourbon.)

Officer's quarters there were in prefab buildings with corrugated metal sides and roofs. Each housed 24 to 32 officers in double-decker bunks, heated by a central coal-fired potbellied stove. Because the Midlands are very cold and damp in winter, I requisitioned extra blankets, folding some double, so I had eight layers to crawl under. They were heavy, but I was reasonably warm. Unfortunately, earlier residents had shot holes in the roof of our building, so rain and snow leaked in.

We spent a week flying around those areas, getting familiar with the terrain, the base location, the wide variety of bad British weather, and where to expect barrage balloons. By then we were deemed ready to go.

OUR FIRST MISSION

The Officers Club had the usual hum of activity until nine in the evening when the jug with the smiling face on the mantel was turned to face the wall, a red light came on, and the bar stopped serving. A mission was scheduled for the next day and our crew would be on it.

Finally I could call myself a "fly boy." I had seen all of the John Wayne movies and other propaganda, so I knew we were the good guys against the bad guys. I was ready to go out and help save the world from the evil empire. At age 19 the thought of injury or death was not a consideration. I felt fatalistic. What was going to happen would happen.

Wake up call came at 3:30 in the morning, breakfast at 4:00, briefing at 4:30. The briefing room was a long building with folding chairs and a raised platform at the end. A map of northern Europe, hidden by a curtain, covered the wall. The briefing officer pulled the curtain back dramatically and a loud groan came from the audience. Our target was to be Nuremberg, about as far into Germany as we could go, with a route that zigzagged diagonally across the country to cause confusion about what would be our ultimate target. We would be flying over Germany for a long time. That was heady stuff for a wet-behind-the-ears 19-year-old.

The separate navigator's briefing was at 5:30 where I was issued maps before I joined the flight line by 6:00 that morning. We picked up our flight gear, parachutes, and escape packages, and reported to our plane. Being the newest crew we were assigned the oldest and coldest B-17 on the base, but we were excited to be flying a real mission at last.

GETTING DRESSED

First we put the flight suit over our uniform wool pants and shirt. It was followed by the electrical suit, the insulated flight jacket, pants, and boots, plus gloves with silk liners. It regularly gets to minus 30 to 50 degrees F at 25-30,000 feet in an un-insulated cabin with undependable heat. The only thing between us and the outside was a thin aluminum skin. Next came the helmet with earphones, throat mike, the "May West" flotation vest, and the parachute harness. Finally the oxygen mask was clipped to the helmet. The whole process took awhile and everything had to be done just so. It is hard to make corrections in the air.

After pulling ourselves up through the front escape hatch (something I could never do today), the pilot, co-pilot, and engineer climbed up to the cockpit while the bombardier and I were in the nose compartment. The radio man, waist gunners, belly gunner, and tail gunner had an easy entrance to the rear of the aircraft behind the bomb bay. It was time to get organized with maps and other items and get plugged-in. The electric suit went into one jack, the nose mike into another, the headset into a third and the oxygen mask hanging from my helmet would go into a fourth when we reached 10,000 feet. With three or four lines connected, I was careful when moving about, but I was able to reach the "cheek" gun across from my navigator's desk in case of fighter attack.

At seven o'clock we rolled onto the taxi strip with other members of our squadron. After takeoff, climbing to higher altitudes, we circled our field numerous times as we formed our squadron and group formations. Through the clouds we could see aircraft from neighboring fields and hoped they were able to keep in their areas of the sky.

After forty minutes of circling we headed for the rendezvous point to join our wing and other groups participating in the mission. With several hundred planes in the air, precision timing is mandatory.

The English Channel looked rough, France itself was quite pretty, and then, after another hour in the air, we entered Germany. During this time we had been escorted by what we called "our little friends," P-51 fighters based in France. But shortly after entering Germany we were on our own. Looking down, the German countryside was peaceful and pastoral with neat farms and small villages appearing from time to time. But we knew we'd meet with hostility if we were forced down.

There were heavy concentrations of antiaircraft guns in the region we were entering and flak darkened the sky. Fortunately we were high enough where most of the guns could not reach us. We then faced flying for more than two hours from the northwest to the southeast of the country, with the threat of fighters all the way.

Finally we saw Nuremberg, surrounded with more antiaircraft guns. We dropped to 23,000 feet in altitude for better bombing accuracy, within range of the guns below. Our target was the railroad marshaling yards on the edge of the city. The dangerous part was the long two- or three-minute bombing run when the plane was under the control of the bombardier. For accurate bombing the plane must be very steady, maintaining constant altitude, speed, and direction. That day everything worked as planned with a good bomb drop.

As we turned away from the target, preparing for our flight home, things changed rapidly. Our far right engine failed and we had to drop out of formation since we could no longer keep up with the other planes. As we watched the rest of the bomber formations head northwest, we headed due west for the nearest friendly area. Within five minutes we lost our far left engine, too. That was not too unexpected since both engines shared many common systems. Flying on two engines meant that we burnt a lot more fuel since the remaining ones were operating at full capacity. If they faltered, we would really be in trouble, forced to crash land or bail out. We would not be able to maintain a safe altitude.

We were able to fly at about 90 mph instead of the normal 170, feeling very much alone and gradually losing altitude. To reduce our weight we threw out all of our extra ammunition, saving only enough for a few short bursts. We were a sitting duck for any German fighter that saw us. Shortly we left the area covered by the maps I had been issued. We just headed west and hoped. Finally we received a response to our distress radio calls and headed for that base. We were down to 10,000 feet by the time we crossed the Rhine, but luck was definitely on our side. We had missed major cities and there was only one antiaircraft gun still shooting at us. Since we were within easy range, he should have been able to pick us off without difficulty. (I think his glasses were broken.) We found out later that our P-47 fighters were strafing the area so most of the enemy guns were quiet.

The field where we were to land was at Etain, France. It was a forward fighter base that had only been established six weeks earlier. The runway was steel mesh spread across the meadow with minimum grading. It wasn't designed to be strong enough, wide enough, or long enough for bombers, so they were justly concerned that our bomber would damage it and their planes wouldn't be able to land there.

With only two engines we had to make it on our first pass. There wouldn't be any more. The bombardier, engineer, and I crawled through the bomb bay and sat down midship with our gunners, bracing ourselves as best we could. Bombers do not have seats and safety belts, except for the pilots. I sat on the metal floor and braced myself against the bulkheads, thanking God for our pilot's experience. He made an excellent landing, slowing down as much as possible, skidding off the end of the runway and across the mud, making one or more out-of-control ground loops before stopping by some bushes. None of us were even badly bruised and we exited very quickly to avoid fire. Our plane did not fare as well. It sat with landing gear destroyed, the propellers bent 90 degrees around the engines, the underbelly bashed in, and one wing severely damaged—a pile of useless metal on the far edge of the field. Our glorious first mission had ended on a damp, cold day with us tramping across a muddy field. It didn't exactly feel like a glorious ending.

In the past, Etain might have been a pretty French village but it had suffered greatly from years of war. The mud on the main road though town was almost up to the top of my flight boots. However, there was still a pretty little white church on the edge of the village where we spent some time. (Etain later became a major American Air Force base and is still in active use as part of NATO.)

The next day we caught the once-a-day flight to Paris which, at the time, was not a very glamorous city and where we were housed in a special hotel the Air Force maintained for escapees and other service people like us. The rooms, like those in all French hotels, contained a bidet. None of us knew what it was for, but we found it very handy for washing our feet.

The weather then closed in, so we ended up spending three nights in Paris in a not very up-scale hotel. This was only a few months after the city had been liberated and there was still the blackout with a nine o'clock curfew for all cafés and businesses.

When the weather finally cleared enough for us to catch a flight to London, a pea-soup fog developed so we had to spend a night there, returning to our base six days after we started our flight. We had left as the newest of new crews and returned as a crew rapidly on our way to becoming veterans.

EPILOG #1

On our next few missions we crash-landed two more times. The first was again due to mechanical failure. We landed at a base in northern France designed for such events, with extra-wide, long runways. After one night there a shuttle flight returned us to our base.

The second occurred when we were hit by flak over Berlin. In a strange way, the deadly pieces of steel flak tearing through our aircraft's aluminum body and wings sounded just like Christmas tree bells or the chime of wine glasses being clinked by happy diners, toasting. Fuel was spewing out of both wings, so our squadron mates asked us to leave the protection of the formation. It looked to them as if we were going to blow up and, if that were so, we ought to do it by ourselves. We flew north over Denmark and then headed on the long trip home diagonally across the North Sea. Since we did not know how much fuel we were losing, we looked at the dark cold water with a great deal of apprehension.

Fortunately we made it all the way back to our base. After firing the warning flares that indicated damage to our plane, we came in for our landing. Fire trucks and ambulances were waiting to chase us down the runway and pick up the pieces. We saw them with mixed feelings: the tower had warned us that only one part of our landing gear was in the down position. As usual, we got into our crash positions, bracing ourselves as best we could. Our pilot made a very skillful landing on the one good wheel, slowing down before a wing touched the ground. We again found ourselves wildly spinning around into the muddy field with several ground loops. Fortunately, no one was injured. Fearing that the plane would burst into flame, we exited quickly and ran across the field.

Our squadron commander later made the comment that our crew had done more to bring in nice new replacement aircraft than anyone else. A very dubious honor!

EPILOG #2

In the mid 1970s, some 25 years after our first mission, I made a business trip to Germany. It was my first since the war and, as fate would have it, my destination was Nuremberg. I traveled with a great deal of apprehension and emotion, arriving on a dark, cold, winter evening and checking into an equally dark, cold, commercial hotel that appeared to be almost empty. Prior to dinner I went into the bar/lounge which was also dark and uninviting. The only people sitting in the lounge area were a couple who left shortly after I arrived. I sat on one of the four bar stools and ordered a beer from the old, grim-faced bartender. As he served the beer, he asked me if I were English. Still very tense and full of apprehension, I said, "No, American, from California." Suddenly his face lit up into a broad smile and he said "I love California!" He had been a prisoner of war in the southern part of the state, in La Jolla. He had been captured in Africa in 1942, was initially sent to Biloxi, then El Paso, and finally to La Jolla. He did not like Biloxi or El Paso at all, but he really loved La Jolla. He continued to talk excitedly, extolling the warm weather, beaches, and fresh fruit. Finally I relaxed.

LIFE AT THE CHILDREN'S COUNTRY SCHOOL

Irving Yabroff

The Children's Country School was a private boarding school founded by two maiden ladies, Mary Orem and her partner, in 1934. Mary Orem was a remarkable person, well educated, and full of innovative ideas on childhood education. The first campus was on Rose Avenue, in Los Gatos in northern California, and consisted of a large residence and a wide open field behind the house. In 1938 the school purchased 14 acres at its present site on Marchmont Drive and by 1960 it had changed its name to the current Hillbrook School and become a day school.

In the beginning, there was a large, three-story family residence, a roomy guest house, a large barn with a wonderful hayloft to play in, and a tall structure which housed a water tank on the top and a pump at the bottom. My mother, brother, and I joined the school family two years after its opening. I was seven years of age and my brother, six. At that time most of the dozen or so other children at the school were wards of the court for which the school received $25 a month for each of them.

Life at The Children's Country School, where I lived until I graduated from high school, was rich and fulfilling. I lived with a group of boys and girls near my age, although I was always one of the oldest. We slept in wooden tents with screening and canvas flaps which we let down when it rained. At six o'clock in the morning, a bell rang and we got up, took off our pajamas, put on our bathrobes and slippers, and ran down to the outside showers protected by a brick wall alongside the swimming pool.

Whichever sex, male or female, got there first went into the cold showers while the others waited in a line outside. We each drank a glass of water before showering. In mid-winter, we would sometimes have to scrape the ice off the shower heads before they would work. I shudder to think of doing that now, but we took it as a matter of course. As a result of this arduous regimen, we seldom had colds.

Each group of about 12 to 16 children had a house-mother or -father who stayed with us 24 hours a day, except for brief periods of an hour or two when we had a substitute. My mother lived with Miss Orem in their own suite of rooms and I seldom saw her. She started out as a secretary, then became business manager and bookkeeper, and much later, after Miss Orem died, became the headmistress.

Schoolwork was fun most of the time. We had small classes ranging from 8 to 15 children. Grades were combined to keep the classes balanced in size. I started out in a class of about 15 students covering grades three through five. As the school grew in attendance and prosperity, we had more teachers and thus fewer combined classes. By the time I reached the eighth grade, my class had eight students who shared a teacher with the seventh grade. The curriculum was very flexible, depending on the desires and imagination of the teacher.

Each winter, the elementary grades would be packed up to go to a snow lodge, usually the one sponsored by the Sierra Club at Norton, California, for a week of classes in the mornings followed by afternoons of skiing.

Year after year the school put on a play at the end of the school terms. All of the children in the upper grades spent one to two hours several times a week memorizing the parts. We were all expected to try out for all of the parts of our gender.

There were always sufficient minor parts so that everyone was in the play, but it wasn't until all the actors for the main parts were chosen that the school got back to a regular schedule. Some of the plays we did were *The Pied Piper of Hamlin* and one about gypsies for which my mother wrote both the words and the songs. As a result of this experience (and a good memory), I can still recite most of the Pied Piper poem and I often find myself humming the songs of the gypsy play. Both of these were particularly gratifying to me because I found that I could recite a memorized part without stuttering. I had a lead role in most of the plays we did.

Miss Orem believed that children could best learn about solving the problems of living by experiencing them at their own level. Thus she formed our own pioneer community within the school which was called "The Village of Friendly Relations." A parcel of ground of about 2000 by 150 feet in the middle of the school grounds was cleared and a circular road marked out. Six buildings were designed by one of the parents who was an architect. These were to be a General Store to sell supplies to the children, a Bank which would issue checks and make loans, a Gift Shop to sell parents the arts and crafts made by the children, a Tea Room which would serve refreshments, a Library to provide books to be borrowed, and a Newspaper Office to issue a weekly school newspaper.

The school maintenance man, who was also a master carpenter, proceeded to construct the foundations and put up the framing. We children were his workers and thus we learned to mix cement, lay bricks for the road, and nail boards and shingles on the sides and roofs. The General Store was built first and Tom, Jim, and I were in charge. We spent many happy hours working on that building after we had finished caring for the school's three Shetland ponies. The General Store had a steeply slanting roof, and it was a real challenge to keep the shingles from sliding to the ground before we could nail them solidly to the boards. Once we had finished the shingling, painting, and nailing the boards on the inside, we were faced with the task of deciding what the store should stock--what the children would like to buy. We conducted a survey and, after it was reviewed by the adults, we were taken to the merchandise distributors to purchase the items. We three ran the store and kept the books for about a year when others were given their chance to do the same.

Ultimately, all buildings but the Library were built and of those built, all but the Tea Room were put into operation and run by us children. My next assignment was the Bank, and I learned my first rudiments of accounting during the year I was bank president, teller, bookkeeper, and janitor.

All decisions about rules of behavior and major design choices were discussed at length and voted upon by the full assembly of the upper grades. We had a regular assembly for this purpose once a week, and special sessions were called when a particularly serious problem arose. Grievance and arbitration procedures were available.

In addition to these planned activities, we also had much free playtime. I have fond memories of many games of *kick-the-can, capture-the-flag,* and *hide-and-seek* using the whole campus to hide in.

In looking back at those seven years of my childhood, I see both the rich community life we children had, as well as the missing pieces of a true family life, especially the lack of individual, intimate, loving contact with a special adult. This lack is typical of institutional living, as well as of many dysfunctional families. The pain of that lack has faded with time and new experiences. But the good times we children had together will always live in strong and happy memories.

A BATTLE IN THE PHILLIPINES

Elsworth Welch

On October 20th of 1944 General Douglas MacArthur made his famous return to the Philippines, landing at Leyte Island. What followed there in the Leyte Gulf on the 24th and 25th of that month was the biggest navel battle ever fought.

In order to defend the Philippines, Admiral Toyoda executed the SHO-GO (Victory Operation) plan, part of which involved several fleets approaching Leyte Island for a pincer attack at the Americans' landing beach. One fleet of battleships slipped through the Surigao Strait south of the island while the other moved through the San Bernardino Strait and swung around Sarmar Island toward Leyte from the north. The latter fleet, made up of four battleships, eight heavy cruisers, and several squadrons of destroyers was under the command of Vice-Admiral Takeo Kurita. As Kurita's force steamed out of San Bernardino Strait toward Samar Island on the morning of October 25th, it was not detected until it encountered a carrier group under the command of Rear Admiral Clifton Sprague. The surprise was mutual.

The Japanese force was spotted by American aviators from the carriers of Taffy 3, one of the several task forces of the 7th Fleet. The Taffy 3 was comprised of six CVEs (Escort Carriers) whose planes were providing support to MacArthur's invasion forces, along with four small destroyer escorts and three destroyers: the USS *Johnston*, USS *Hoel*, and the USS *Heerman*. Admiral Sprague was aboard the *Fanshaw Bay*, one of the carriers. When he heard the report of the sighting of the Japanese fleet, he ordered his ships to turn to an easterly windward course, away from the enemy. He needed help from the other two Taffy forces, but he knew that they were a long way off. Taffy 3 was the closest to the enemy's position.

As a young ensign, I had been assigned to a destroyer, the *USS Johnston* when it was put into commission in Seattle on October 27, 1943 under the command of Captain Ernest Evans, a Cherokee Indian and a graduate of the U. S. Naval Academy in Annapolis. During World War II the *Johnston* was engaged in many naval battles in the Pacific, but its last battle took place off Samar Island in the Leyte Gulf, there in the Philippine Sea.

It was on the morning of October 25th at 6:25 when General Quarters sounded aboard the *USS Johnston* and Captain Evans' voice came over the speaker.

"Units of the enemy fleet are 15 miles astern. All hands to General Quarters. Prepare to attack major portions of the Japanese fleet. All engines head flank. Commence making smoke and stand by for torpedo attack. Left full rudder."

That attack was a case of little David against Goliath. (But in the Bible story David won!) Vice-Admiral Kurito's *Yamata* was the largest battleship every built. Each of her main gun turrets weighed more than all the guns on the three destroyers in Taffy 3. The Japanese battleships could fire shells more than 26 miles. Among the thirteen ships of Taffy 3 there wasn't a gun larger than five inches. The 54-pound shells they fired had a range of about seven miles and could not penetrate battleship armor.

After the crew had secured from General Quarters, I resumed the deck watch which, up to then for me, was routine. About 6:45 I was leaning over the port side of the bridge, smelling delightful breakfast odors wafting up from the galley. Suddenly the dullness disappeared. Huge geysers of salt water were thrown up near the carriers. I looked up for enemy planes, but realized that our radar would have detected the aircraft. I dashed to the starboard side and saw, coming out of a rain squall, an enemy fleet, hull down over the horizon. The Japanese had gotten within gun range by the time word came over the TBS that we were being attacked by a major portion of the enemy fleet. Commander Evans ordered the engine room to light all boilers to make funnel smoke and our smoke screen generator detail to make chemical smoke which would hide us.

The pagoda masts of the Japanese battleships, first observed on the horizon at 17 miles distance, were closing in rapidly at 22 to 25 knots when our carriers had a maximum speed of about 18 knots. Then the Japanese fleet closed in more slowly. Perhaps Admiral Kurita thought that our formation consisted of large carriers, cruisers, and destroyers. We were in range of their large guns; there were splashes around our carriers. We zigzagged a smoke barrier between the enemy and our formation. At that time we were the closest ship to the enemy. By visual observation and our surface radar, the count was four Japanese battleships, four-to-six cruisers, and ten-to-twelve destroyers. When the enemy fleet came within our gun range, Bob Hagen, our gun boss, opened fire. All ten torpedoes were launched. I saw one of them hit the Japanese cruiser's fantail with an enormous explosion. As we rejoined our formation, we took a number of hits, wiping out one engine and one boiler room, the gyro compass, and most of the electrical power. We could barely make 16 knots.

During the run-in I was on the port wing of the bridge with Lieutenant Ed Digardi, Bechdel, and the captain, who gave orders for a course change. I went into the pilot house with Digardi and about ten seconds later we took our first hits. A battleship salvo (three 14 inches) hit the after-engine and fire rooms, followed by a six-incher salvo which hit the port wing of the bridge. When we returned to the bridge, it was in carnage. Bechdel was propped against the wheel house, complaining about injuries to his arms, not aware that his legs were blown off. To relieve his pain, I gave him morphine before medics arrived to remove the dead and dying. The recognition officer has lost his head, others were wounded, and the captain had shrapnel wounds to his hand, neck, and chest. It was a grizzly sight. Pieces of bodies were strewn over the deck. Such a sight would not help morale, so I tended the living wounded and tossed these bits of the dead and dying overboard.

Our ship was dead in the water, had lost steering engine power, and could only communicate with steering aft by phone. The crew at the rudder had to operate the rudder hydraulic system by hand.

Finally we turned and, under cover of smoke, again headed south. The *Hoel* (destroyer) was sunk, the *Roberts* (destroyer escort) was sunk, and the *Heerman* (destroyer) had moved away, unscathed and at full power. The *Gambier Bay* (carrier) was damaged and taking heavy fire, then listed to port and sank.

The captain ordered what was left of the pilothouse crew to go to the fantail where he directed the firing of the only remaining gun maneuvering the ship. When it stopped firing he ordered me to find out why. I made my way through choking smoke and over piles of dead bodies. The captain and I were on opposite sides of the bridge, moving toward it but when I arrived there it was abandoned. Fifteen minutes later I joined him on the fantail. A seaman and I dumped depth charges which might go off when the ship sank (one did) while the captain chased shell flashes, a maneuver to avoid the ship's being hit.

The *Johnston* was slowing and useless. Captain Evans ordered, "All hands abandon ship!" That was the last I saw of him. I went forward, repeating his order. Debris and fires were everywhere. To abandon ship, we had been taught to jump into the water feet first to avoid hitting our heads on debris. However, I am a swimmer and diver, so I took off my shoes, placed them neatly together to leave them behind, and dove a few feet into the sea. Since the ship was sinking, I swam rapidly away and inflated my life belt. Shells were falling all around me, and I was struck with my head out of the water like a diving duck. Survivors in the water were beginning to gather together. The Japanese fleet had headed north and we were left alone.

That night a terrifying experience occurred to me. I felt something grab the back of my life belt, ripping it and tearing off the seat of my pants and shorts. This was a situation for which I wasn't prepared. My contract with the Navy was to fight the enemy, not sharks. I soon found a life jacket floating in the water to replace my lost life belt. There were sharks all around us. Some survivors of the *Johnston* were on two rafts; others were on floater nets. Several, like me, were attacked by sharks.

After three hours of battle, Admiral Sprague got the astonishing news that Kurita's fleet was withdrawing and turning north, into the open sea toward Japan. Apparently his ships had been battered enough by the Americans that he assumed he was facing a formidable foe. He felt he could not enter Leyte Gulf to attack MacArthur's landing beach because his force had become strung out during the battle and scattered in some thirty miles of ocean. The *Yamato* had turned north to avoid torpedoes from the American destroyers.

The next day, after we abandoned ship, we still had our hopes up that we would be rescued. We had gone down over the Mindanao Trench, the deepest spot in the Pacific, five miles down and about 60 or 70 miles off Samar. By the second day afloat we had finished the last of our rations, including a few malted milk tablets, some Spam, and some water which was stale because no one had replaced the water on the rafts during our months at sea.

The second night was a disaster. Dehydration and exposure to the sun were threats to our lives. Men were drinking sea water and going crazy. During the night we all took turns sleeping and staying awake to keep the others from sliding off. The badly wounded died and were set adrift. The weaker among us began to hallucinate from fatigue. Some of them slipped off the raft after seeing visions of home, native girls on shore, or coffee in the wardroom. Ed Digardi and I spent most of the night shepherd-dogging the group, pulling back persons drifting away, and tying them to a floater net. Even today I feel badly that I was too exhausted to stop some who floated off by themselves.

By the next morning, the third day, we could see land a few miles away and hear the breaking surf. I wanted to swim to the beach, but we decided that we should stay put. In the early afternoon we spotted a rescue ship, an LCI (Landing Craft). The crew threw over a cargo net and we climbed aboard.

The ships that rescued us were part of a task group of the Leyte amphibious landing force. They had left Leyte on the day of the battle and moved west toward Samar in a search formation, slowly picking their way through the sea at just 10 knots, their top speed. An officer on the deck of one of the ships saw red, white, and green flares about 20 miles ahead to port. After some confusion, the skipper agreed that the flares were probably American. On the morning of October 27 they retrieved survivors of the *Gambier Bay*. The LCTs continued searching and, about five hours later, we survivors of the *Johnston* and those of the *Hoel* were found.

During the battle, Taffy 3 had been the first victim of Japanese *kamikaze* attacks. Two *kamikazes* attacked the *Fanshaw Bay* but were knocked off before they could hit. But the *St Lo* wasn't so lucky. A Zero fighter plane, bombs under each wing, plunged into its flight deck and, falling below decks, ignited the ammunition stored below. The ship went down fast. Other ships of Taffy 3, near the scene, recovered the survivors. Admiral Sprague was successful in rescuing the victims closest to him, but relied on other task forces to search for survivors in distant areas. There was a communication problem within the 7th Fleet. If pilots had spotted Taffy 3 survivors, the reports were not relayed.

After the war, the Japanese Navy Minister told MacArthur that the Japanese defeat at Leyte was "tantamount to the loss of the Philippines. When you took the Philippines, that was the end of our resources."

MY ROLE AS A MODEL

Janet Rafferty

Sometime in early May of 1953, I got a letter saying that I had won the Mademoiselle Magazine Guest Editor Contest which I had entered the previous September. That letter made a great change in my life. I was never dependent on my family again, but at the time that was not my intention. I was going away, but I wanted to go back home to work the rest of the summer when the magazine job was over at the end of June. I wanted to return to Knox College in the fall and graduate with my class. But in my excited state, planning to go to New York, I never thought that far ahead.

My mother was very emotional at our parting, crying on my father's shoulder even though we all expected that I would only be gone a month and I was already 22 years old. I left on a CB & Q train early the morning of June 1 and, after the four-hour ride, got off with my one jammed suitcase and a large equally jammed handbag at Chicago's Grand Central Station where I hailed a cab for the airport. It was to be my first flight. Jets had not yet been invented or, at least, were not in use, and I got an old-fashioned American Airlines plane for another four-hour trip to La Guardia Airport in New York City. I had been warned that, if no one met me, I should take a cab to the Barbizon Hotel for Women on 63rd Street and Lexington Avenue. I was fed on both the train and the plane and was so tired from all the commotion and noise at the airports that I went straight to the hotel, asked for my room which was ready on the seventh floor, and collapsed.

The next day I met Sylvia Plath, like me one of three recipients of a first prize in the Mademoiselle contest. We ate breakfast downstairs in the hotel, met all the other winners, and walked over to our first day on the job at 575 Madison Avenue. Sylvia had won first prize in poetry and fiction-writing; I had won in the nonfiction/essay category. Another young women named Eileen McLaughlin won a first in art. There were also 17 other winners in these three categories. Every day was a flurry of activity and the month literally whizzed by.

Imagine my surprise when I received a letter from home saying that all the possible jobs for me in Galesburg were gone and I should stay in New York for the rest of the summer and find work there! But when I inquired about jobs, no one in the city was willing to hire me for just two months. The last week that I was at Mademoiselle a trustee of my college and friend of my parents, Willard Dean, asked me out to lunch. He took me to the world-famous Stork Club. There at a nearby table was a woman whom I later learned was Eileen Ford. She came over to our table, gave me her card, and started talking about a job for me as a model at her agency. She asked me to come up to her agency the day after the July 4th weekend. Mr. Dean had heard of her and encouraged me to accept her offer.

I had no idea what I would do there or even what models did all day. I just thought how nice it was that my problem was solved. I had my return plane ticket home and $50 left of my prize money. That was all. I put up a notice that I needed a place to rent and got a reply from Rachel Melinger who had worked fulltime at Mademoiselle since she graduated from Radcliffe the June before. Rachel had a room for $5 a week. It was a five-flight walk-up, but in the Gramercy Park area of the city which was considered a good neighborhood. I would have two roommates, Rachel and another recent college grad named Beth who worked as an intern at CBS. July 4th was a Monday that year so the last day at the magazine and the Barbizon Hotel (which was paid for) was the Thursday before. That Barbizon was very costly. For the small cell-like room and a bath to share down the hall, Mademoiselle paid $25 a day. (Today that hotel is still there at 63rd and Lexington Avenue, greatly remodeled and the rooms, all with private baths, start at $350 per day.)

So on the last day of June I moved with the small black suitcase from home, plus a large brown cardboard box tied up with some rope, into my first independent living situation, arriving there in a cab paid for out of the $50 I had left. Work started at Eileen Ford's on Tuesday, the 5th. In the meantime I was all alone in the big apartment. My roommates had come from the New York City suburbs and gone home to their families for the holiday. At first I loved the space I had. So much better than being cooped up at the Barbizon! But it was also terribly lonely. I missed all the things my family and I had done together on the 4th in the past. I bought eggs, milk, mayonnaise, and bread because they were cheap. I boiled the eggs and made egg salad sandwiches which, as it turned out, I lived on for at least a month.

On Tuesday Eileen Ford said that I would not be able to work right away. She gave me a map of New York City, bought me some pancake makeup, and introduced me to my first model friend, Lorriane Davies. Lorriane spent the afternoon showing me how to put on the pancake makeup. I have never forgotten her kindness and she has remained a life-long friend. We never worked together because, while she was extremely beautiful, she was only five-feet, five and one-half inches tall. She wore heels all the time and

Eileen told her to tell clients that she was five-feet, six-inches tall. When she measured me and discovered that I was a quarter of an inch over five feet, nine inches, Eileen told me never to tell anyone that I was more than five feet, nine inches tall.

I was given a list of photographers to see who, free of any charge, would take photos of me. Eileen told me to quit smiling. I soon discovered that I didn't like "high fashion," kept on smiling, and found my own clients who liked that. She introduced me to a former model named Lily Carlson who was starting out as a photographer. She was from Kewanaee, Illinois, near my hometown, Galesburg. She lent me clothes for the shoots and gave me her nice apartment for the whole month of August while she went to Europe with David, her fiancé. I cashed in my plane ticket home and bought a portfolio for the photographs taken of me.

Eileen didn't think that I was ready to work yet, so Lily sent me to another agency, Frances Gill. Right away I got a job in Detroit doing Mercury car ads. That was my first big job: I got $100 a day for six days! My employers put me up in a nice hotel and paid for all my expenses.

I intended to go home from there and found out that I could buy a train ticket from Detroit to Galesburg for about $50. I decided I would have to borrow that $50 because all my other money was gone. One day I steeled myself to ask for that money from the person who sat next to me on the train I was taking from a beach town in Long Island where I had gone with some new friends. The man sitting next to me looked like he might lend me the money, so I asked him. He was startled, but took out his wallet and gave it to me. I told him that I could repay it as soon as the job was over and I got my $600. He handed me his card with his work address where he was selling Rolls Royce cars at their showroom on Park Avenue. He told me later, when I had paid him back, that he never expected to see that money again. His name was Eddie Collins and, yes, he did sell Rolls Royces on Park Avenue.

The photographer for the Detroit job was a professor at Michigan State University. He and his wife entertained me and spent the entire week convincing me that I should not return home, but instead go back to New York City and continue a career as a model. I ended up taking their advice: I got an advance on the $600, enrolled in New York University night school, got a room in its nearby women's dormitory, and continued working for the Frances Gill Agency. Of course I had to see Eileen and quit her agency. She yelled at me so hard and was so enraged that I was glad to be out of there. But, still, she had gotten me started with the portfolio of photographs. Doing my senior year at night took two more years instead of one, but I was graduated in 1955. Henry Cabot Lodge spoke at my graduation and I had a new husband in the audience.

I remember many things about those years of modeling, but two incidents particularly stand out. The first had to do with Gloria Steinam whom I met soon after I arrived in New York City in June of 1953 to work for Mademoiselle Magazine. I admired her because she was trying to make a living in the city by writing. We were both about 22 years old.

I had a booking at a photo studio downtown near where I lived at 4 East 10th Street. The photographer, who looked like the young actor, Toby Maguire, was someone I'd never worked for before, so the ad agency had probably suggested me. Gloria was working there as his assistant and stylist. She and I said "Hello!" to each other before I entered the dressing room. I don't really know how much she knew about me, but I think she did know that I was from the Midwest and maybe that I was a winner of the Mademoiselle contest. As soon as we started shooting, she started a three-way conversation including both me and the photographer. (This is sometimes done to relax the model so the photos will look more natural and not posed.)

I've forgotten what the photographer said, but I remember Gloria's suddenly saying—as if to me—"Well, I don't think a woman's virginity is worth enough to be saved." I was shocked and, although I knew that she was probably doing it to get a rise out of me, she got it. I answered her by saying, "But sex creates life. It's a sacred act." I don't remember anything else about the job except another model in the dressing room afterwards told me that Gloria had moved in with that photographer. That explained why the atmosphere in the whole studio became quiet and uncomfortable after I spoke. Nothing more was said and I left. I did work there again once, but Gloria was gone.

Later I took another kind of stand at a fitting in a cheap dress factory over in the 7th Avenue area. I worked over there every season for BH Wragge. I did his shows when the big store buyers came into town. Designers had one or two "fit models" who worked on salaries and did not make as much money as those of us who did photography and worked through an agency. The really cheap houses didn't even hire a fit model and, if we were booked for a magazine ad, the fitting would have to be at their business. I had never before been in one of these lower echelon factories.

I entered a huge room, wall-to-wall with little women sewing furiously at little machines. They were all Puerto Ricans. (The better houses used Italians, mostly women, and the very high-end ones like Galanos used French seamstresses.) I threaded my way through them to the center where there was standing one of the biggest, tallest, black-haired, meanest-looking men I had ever seen. He was motioning me to him. I introduced myself. He handed me a dress on a hangar and told me to put it on. I asked where the dressing room was. He stood very near me and said in a loud voice right in my face, "Who do you think you are? The VIRGIN MARY?"

I never moved. Thoughts raced through my mind. *He thinks I'm a Catholic. I can't say I'm not a Catholic. Maybe he thinks all Christians are Catholics.* Suddenly I noticed the total quiet in the room. All the sewing machines had stopped. I still said nothing. I was scared stiff. I could not move; I could not talk. I was paralyzed.

Somewhere in that huge room two little hands started to clap. Then the whole room erupted with wild applause. I knew for a moment what it felt like to be a diva at the Met. He quickly turned away from me, saying, "Okay, you won." Then he told a young male worker, José, to go get a roll of fabric in the corner. José got the cloth and draped it over the overhead pipes. The mean man got me a folding chair and hung a dirty mirror on a pillar. "There's your dressing room." He disappeared. An elderly lady came and pinned the dress in all the right places. I re-dressed; he signed my voucher to pay me for a half-hour fitting, and I left. But I never did the job. He cancelled the photography shoot with me and got another model.

That incident changed me forever. Afterwards, I always said, "Good morning" or "Good afternoon" to those little ladies at the sewing machines when I had to walk through their space. I never forgot how important they were to me that day. I understand now the Puerto Rican seamstresses are the best in New York and work only for the high-end designers.

Who is working now in all the sweat shops of the low-end fashions? I'm sure they are still there. But I believe that mean-looking man was right about the Virgin Mary. She would not have taken her clothes off in front of a strange man.

IF I ONLY UNDERSTOOD THEN…

Bill Murphy

If I only understood then what I understand now! It was June of 1952 and little did I know that the next 12 months would serve as the defining year of my entire life, both personally and professionally.

In early 1952 my father, a career Army officer, received orders to SHAPE (Supreme Allied Headquarters Europe) which was situated in France. He was to precede my mother, my two sisters, my brother, and me to this assignment by a few months. This would allow him to find housing, locate schools, and arrange the myriad of things necessary to make the family's arrival relatively free of chaos. However, despite all preparation, these repeated moves were always accompanied by a mixture of anticipation, trauma, good and bad surprises, fear, stress, and delight. I should have been used to them by that time, since I had already accompanied my family to several of my father's wide-ranging military assignments, but the prospect of this particular move was extremely difficult for me.

I was to enter my senior year of high school that fall. I had attended four high schools as a result of family moves and had already established myself as an incoming senior at Serra High School in San Mateo, California. All I held dear at the age of 16 was there: the friends, the sports, and the social life. Faced with a new switch, I decided to exercise my version of teenage resistance, an attribute not tolerated with any great enthusiasm by my parents. In order to function in our fast moving military environment, the family needed to function as a cohesive unit. Suddenly, the oldest son announced his intention to remain stateside with relatives and friends. After patiently listening to my case for remaining behind, my father carefully took each of my points and persuaded me to re-evaluate them. His closing argument went something like, "In my absence, I *expect* you to accompany your mother, sisters and younger brother on the long trip across country and overseas." Confronting me with that logic, his declarative appeal to my responsibility as the oldest son was the clincher. I don't recall ever bringing up the subject again.

My father departed for France and the rest of us went about preparing for the upcoming trip, waiting for my Dad to call and give us the signal to be on our way. I did find time to play a lot of baseball (a year-round passion) and to say proper goodbyes to friends. We had been through these periodic farewells many times before. They were typical rituals all military families face. But this one was different. For the first time we were headed outside the United States! This time, for us, there was a heavy air of anticipation and, as it turned out, we were not to be disappointed.

My Dad called for us to proceed in early July. Travel plans were set and, before we knew it, we were on a train heading from California, bound for New York. It must have been difficult for my Mom, but she was so incredibly strong and organized that she was well-equipped to shepherd all four of her children on our journey. The four-day ride was an adventure for my siblings and me, one ending with my lifelong romance with trains. When we pulled into Grand Central Station, we were met and escorted to Fort Hamilton to wait with other military dependents for our designated air transportation to Europe. That would be on commercial flights contracted by the government to transport military dependents around the world. Waiting for our flight seemed to take forever, but I am told it only took a few days. It was finally called and we packed up once again. At La Guardia we boarded a four-engine propeller-driven aircraft full of women and children all bound for Europe and reunions with their spouses and fathers.

The trip took 17 hours with one stop in Gander, Newfoundland. We eventually landed in Frankfurt, Germany, and went from there by train to Paris, France. Everything was new, strange, and exciting, but nothing matched our collective delight when Dad met us at the Gare de Lyon station. He made me especially proud when he thanked me for acting in his stead and shook my hand with an accompanying look that said more than words could express. If I had only understood then what I understand now!

My father's specific assignment was near Fontainebleau, a town about 60 kilometers southeast of Paris. While the final arrangements for our permanent home were being completed, we lived temporarily in a house near the center of the town. Before a couple of months had passed, we had moved to the rural community of Marlotte and settled into a large farmhouse in the midst of a beautiful forest. The accommodations included a live-in housekeeper named Denise. This remarkable 60-year-old woman had been a decorated French Resistance fighter during World War II--all 4 feet 10 inches of her! She spoke no English and made it clear that she had no intention of learning it. Rather, she took it upon herself to teach us all French. Her charm, smile, and unflagging spirit were gifts she gave us that we would cherish the rest of our lives. Three years later, my parents tried to convince Denise to come back to the United States as part of our family. She declined, saying she didn't have either the right shoes or the right accent.

With the extraordinary help of Denise, and the bond she forged with my mother, we all quickly settled into our new environment. My Dad had already registered all of us in school. My older sister was off to college in Munich, Germany, at an extension of the University of Maryland. I was enrolled as a senior in a high school in Paris, and my younger siblings were scheduled to attend local French schools. (Later they would relate that experience as one of the most memorable of their lives.)

I had to leave home at about 5:30 each morning to catch the military bus which took 10 or so dependents from Fontainebleau and environs to Paris. Our school, Paris American High School (PAHS), was one of several established in Europe by the Department of Defense providing military dependents with a reasonable facsimile of a stateside education. The school, now the Iraqi Embassy, was located at 53 Rue de la Faisanderie in the heart of Paris. The building was originally a four-story home on one of the streets radiating from the Arch de Triumph and our teenage hangout was the American Embassy not far away. We all soon became expert in the use of the Paris metro.

There were 15 students in my graduating class from PAHS. Since we were all sons and daughters of the military with obviously similar backgrounds, we immediately established a bond that is unbroken to this day. The group of us naturally formed the nucleus of every activity offered at the school. We soon discovered that acting together brought out the best in each other. This discovery manifested itself in academics, sports, social events, or student government.

Through a process I don't remember, I was selected as student council president of the total enrollment of just over 100 students. One of the duties that council was charged with was student discipline. When a student violated a school rule, the council determined and applied the sentence of punishment. It was my unpleasant duty to hand down suspensions to a group of junior girls caught smoking on a school balcony. One of these culprits was Jean Early. She was none too happy with my harsh judgment. As a matter of fact, I was to marry this young woman nine years later and, to this day, she occasionally reminds me of my "miscarriage of justice!"

If I had only understood then what I understand now!

Despite that rough beginning to our relationship, I soon fell under Jean Early's spell and courted her for the remainder of my senior year. Our first date was the Christmas dance. I made some awkward approach to ask her and she, fortunately, accepted or I probably would have been too discouraged to ask her out again. After the dance we ventured into the night life of the city and ended up at The Crazy Horse Saloon where we were treated to the incredible singing voice of a waif of a woman named Edith Piaf. Jean also celebrated her 16th birthday that year and her father arranged a memorable dinner for all of her friends at the Café de Paris. I had never attended such an elaborate birthday party! He had reserved the entire second floor of this world-famous restaurant complete with a seven-course meal and strolling violin players.

If only I understood then what I understand now!

It was shortly after Christmas of 1952 and this remarkable year was about half over. Winter had set in and my life was a continuous cycle of early mornings, long bus rides, and hectic school activities filled with speculation about what the future held for each of us. I spent a great deal of my time that winter trying to find every approach to convince my Mom and Dad to let me stay in Paris on the weekends. Inventing any excuse I could devise, I pleaded with them to let me stay overnight with friends. When all else failed, I tried to gain their sympathy by stating that my love life was in serious jeopardy because Jean lived in Paris and could not be expected to be my "steady" if I could not see more of her. My parents remained steadfast! I was not allowed to roam free in the City of Lights.

There is sometimes very little difference between divine intervention and parental guidance. Without my knowledge my Mom and Dad had taken time to contact Jean's father (a single parent) and gotten to know and like him. My parents had become acquainted with Jean, too, and felt the same way about her. At this juncture, serious conversations began between them and me. They insisted that I concentrate on my future education. They were very reassuring that a future relationship between Jean and me would be fine by them, but thought that, for now, my priority should be getting myself prepared for life after high school. My Dad said he would help me as best he could, but the major financial burden would have to be mine. College without a full scholarship (or partial scholarship and a job) was therefore out of the question.

Then, by a stroke of genius (which I had become accustomed to from my Mom or Dad), my father offered the perfect solution. Over the next few months he would help me prepare for entrance exams to all the military academies and, if I were not selected for one of the entering classes of 1953, I could still enlist in the Army and retake the exams the following year. Since the academies indeed offered a four-year scholarship, if I were not selected and needed to do a tour in the Army while drawing an enlisted man's pay, I could apply again the next year. The problem was essentially solved! The logic was undeniable and I wholeheartedly agreed.

If only I understood then what I understand now!

The next few months (from January to May of 1953) were the most intense periods of study I had ever undertaken. Besides my regular school load, I spent the majority of evenings and nights taking correspondence courses in math, science, and English, preparing myself for the upcoming entrance exams to the various American military academies. In reality, those exams were a competition for an appointment from my senator or congressperson. In addition, I could compete for a presidential appointment as the son of a regular Army officer. My Dad was equal to his word. He endured my complaining, helped me with difficult test problems, kept me physically fit by insisting upon a regular workout routine, and coaxed me when I felt discouraged. My Mom supplied moral support, as only a mother can, and worked hard to minimize distractions. She set up a room in the attic which became my study. Everyone became involved in my quest, including Denise, who got up with me at five o'clock every weekday morning and fed me like a king, encouraging me incessantly in her rambling French.

May arrived quickly and I was off to take the entrance exams at a military facility in Hamburg, Germany. There were several young men taking the exams with me from military families stationed around Europe. To say I was prepared is an understatement. All those hours in the attic study room must have paid off because I don't remember the exams being terribly difficult. In addition to math, science and English exams, I had to take a series of physical tests that included running for time, pull-ups, pushups, sit-ups and sprints. After a couple of days, I returned home to France to await the outcome.

There were other classmates of mine who had better grades than I did that senior year but, based upon cumulative grade point average over four years of high school, I was selected as class valedictorian. My address to the gathered assembly at graduation in early June allowed me to thank my parents for all they had done for me and to say goodbye to my classmates who would scatter throughout the world within a few weeks. I hadn't heard from any of the academies, so I expected to enlist shortly thereafter and return to the States for boot camp. We were all laughing and shaking hands after the formal ceremony when Jean and I saw Mom and Dad approaching with smiles that only proud parents seem to muster. The next moments are forever frozen in my memory. My parents hugged me as if it would be the last embrace for quite a while. It was then that my Dad told me that I had been accepted at the Naval Academy that same morning. In fact, I had to report for my plebe year the following week. At that point in time my professional life was firmly established.

A few months later Jean's Dad retired and moved their home to Baltimore. She had to finish another year of high school and then attended Randolph Macon Woman's College in Lynchburg, Virginia. Five years passed. We both graduated from college and started our respective careers, Jean as a teacher and I as a military officer. We dated periodically for another three years and Jean finally decided that I was worth the risk and agreed to spend the rest of her life with me. Our marriage was simply the end result of a relationship that began in that magical year in Paris. My personal life had also been firmly established at that point in time!

My military career was incredibly fulfilling and, together, Jean and I raised six remarkable children. If I had prevailed in early 1952 and my parents had relented and left me behind when they moved to France, my personal and professional lives would certainly have been entirely altered. So now I *do* understand what I didn't understand then. Most of all that knowledge has to do with the outcome of parenting. The influence of those two people can be a major factor in determining a child's future. Their encouragement and support help immensely in the growth of their offspring. I also understand how important teenage relationships can be when they are nurtured and allowed to mature as mine was. And how outside influences can play dramatic roles in everyone's life. There are literally hundreds of instances that we consider insignificant at the time of their occurrence that determine the shape of our lives. In my case, all the forces of parental influence, luck, fate, and destiny seemed to be aligned in the months from June 1952 to June 1953. That year defined the rest of one adolescent Irishman's life and I will be forever grateful for it.

THE LONER

Barnet Greene

Both my father and my mother were brought up in very tight financial circumstances and had to go to work when they were still children. My own childhood was an echo of those hard times.

In 1923, when I was seven years old, my parents bought a house in Brooklyn. This two-family building sheltered my parents, my two brothers, Edward and Jerry, myself, and the family downstairs. At that time the section of Brooklyn where we lived was moving from agricultural to residential in an area including everything from Prospect Park to the beaches.

The section of Brooklyn that I knew was made up of families of European immigrants. The children were all my friends. I couldn't go out of the house without tripping on them. But there were no Blacks, no Asians, and no Hispanics. The city jobs were divided; the Italians were the garbage men, the Jews, the teachers, and the Irish the police and firemen. All together, in our Brooklyn, they were called the "Triple I League" for Italy, Israel, and Ireland.

My education started out in what was still a country school, made up of four separate classroom and office buildings, plus another one for the washroom. All of these were connected by boardwalks to keep us out of the seasonal mud. By October, every day we boys were pulling on boots and tucking our knickers into them. We didn't give up that protection until April. Our winter caps came with earmuffs, but the catch was that, if you took the muffs out and actually used them to cover your ears to keep them warm, of course you couldn't hear the teachers. The winters were so cold and our classroom heating so inadequate that we kept our overcoats on whenever we were inside the building. There were too many students, and somewhere in the middle of the room was only one round-bellied stove which didn't provide enough heat to keep all forty of us warm. Outside temperatures from zero to 15 degrees were not uncommon.

After two years in the country school, we pupils were moved into a new five-floor building. It had an elevator but that was only for the use of teachers and disabled students. There were separate showers for boys and girls at the gym which, like the auditorium, was connected to the main building. Those were used a lot because we knew that hot-water showers at home were expensive.

I was a lonesome boy and in grammar school I read a lot, especially history. When I graduated, to my surprise I was awarded the American Legion's history medal. My parents never said anything about it, so I thought it couldn't have been very important to them. It was money that mattered, money that we didn't have. The Great Depression hit soon after that and I got a newspaper route because then there wasn't money for anything, not even new shoes. I covered my worn-out ones with rubbers to keep the rain from coming through to my socks.

My parents weren't very serious about their boys being raised Jewish. However, when I was 13, I was *bar mitzvahed* in a Reform temple. After that I didn't attend a *shull* until I got married. The closest I got to my religion was during my four years of military service when I had the burning faith to ask God to help me come out alive. Since I was more or less brought up a Jewish child, the idea of Christian Christmas was a strange one. At that time of year, when I delivered my newspapers, my Christian customers gave me a dollar or two--tips which were unheard of sums of money to me. It was a wonderful introduction to peace on earth, good will to men! How can I describe what I bought! It included a bicycle, baseball bats, ice hockey skates, tennis rackets, and sneakers for myself and the brother next to me in age. That was paradise enough but, since I sold a lot of newspapers, I also got a reward--a ticket to the Yankee Stadium to see Babe Ruth!

Another benefit from my three years of having a newspaper route was the development of a strong right arm from throwing the papers onto the porches every day. I discovered how strong it was when I started playing handball on an open court. (The four-walled ones had a gymnasium smell built in, so I never liked using them.) At ten I shouldn't have been where I was when I was hit by a baseball bat. The ambulance came and took me, yelling and screaming to the hospital where they sewed me up. I still have the scar.

The Brooklyn Navy Yard doesn't exist anymore, but when I was very young my brothers and I used to go there onto the ships, go down into the submarine, raise the periscope, and see the outside world.

We didn't go anywhere with our parents after we were about 11 if we could get out of it, but before that, Memorial Day was a special occasion since my father took us out to see the parade, first of Civil War veterans, then the Spanish-American War vets, and after that, the First World War veterans. I didn't want to be a soldier; I didn't want to have a rifle. Little did I know that later I would be in the service and have three rifles and a bayonet.

When I was 11, I saw Charles Lindbergh waving to us from his open car on King's Highway. We were celebrating his successful flight to Paris. At 12 I was old enough to join the Boy Scouts and go to my first Brooklyn Boy Scouts Camp. That camp was on thousands of acres in the Delaware Water Gap area and all together held about 1,200 boys. We went at least three hours away from New York City by train. There were two lakes for swimming, canoeing, and boating. We took overnight trips and played all kinds of sports. I loved it. It was wonderful! Partly because there were NO PARENTS! (But when we went in for the evening meal, we had to show a postcard we'd written to our parents: "I'm fine. Having a wonderful time! Love to everybody!") As I grew older, I ended up going to those camps three times.

I used to go with my brothers every Saturday to see silent films starting at 12:30. They were all cowboy movies and, when the cowboy hero shot the villain, every one of the 500 boys in the audience shot off his cap gun, too. We each took an apple, a pear, or a banana with us because we didn't have the money to buy the food that was sold in the movie house. About 7:30 our father came, calling out our names so we'd go home with him.

At 13 in high school I discovered girls. VIVA LA DIFFERENCE! We couldn't drive so we walked to the movies. There was a movie house every ten streets. By that time the expensive theaters had a series of vaudeville acts, Pathé or Fox news, as well as the talkies that repeated during the day.

When I was 16, on Thanksgiving Day the three sisters (my mother and the other two) prepared the meal for the whole family. We six boys didn't do anything to help, just ran around chasing each other and hitting out at each other. That was the way boys behaved.

At 18 you could smoke, drive a car, and date girls, but for me by the time I reached that age, any ease left of my boyhood was gone. I had to go to work fulltime. The Depression was fierce. It was many years later that, with the help of the G. I. Bill I finally got my college education at American University and found my life's work in accounting. That was an occupation that was easy for me and a pleasure.

EMERGENCY AT SEA

Norman Gould

Sometimes long delays in being served in our communal dining room bring out good stories swapped across our tables. One evening not too long ago the delays were so long that we joked that the cooks were tending the gardens, picking the produce for the meal we were waiting for.

Being slow at doing some things may be a widespread, consistent human frailty. Thoughts about another frailty, one that had come to me as something of a surprise jostled my mind. That was the desire some of us have to show off, to prove some special capability. I was remembering when I had a particularly vivid experience of that.

Years ago I entered the Navy during peacetime because I expected that one day Uncle Sam would probably exact ten pounds of flesh in the form of public service for putting me through pre-med and medical school at no cost to me. After my internship at the Naval Hospital in Long Beach, California, I opted to spend another two years in the Navy. The day after I finished that internship, I was immediately assigned as a medical officer to the *USS Bayfield, APA 33,* based in Norfolk, Virginia. Periodically our fleet went for four or five days at a time, performing assault exercises of the type likely to be used if there were future wars.

One early morning, as I was indulging myself in some "sack" time, I received a radio call from one of the other ships taking part in the same exercises. The call was from the medical officer on that ship who was requesting that I come aboard to consult with him concerning one of the sailors who was complaining about a severe pain in his right lower quadrant. The radioed request was phrased as a demand; I had to respond. I didn't want to go, but obviously I had to. It was not the day for a joy ride. The seas were threatening and I was apprehensive.

That meant that I had to go from my ship to his in terrible, terrible seas. That was a journey I still remember very well. First of all, I had to get a crew together to take me to the other ship, men who would use a crane to lower a boat from our ship to the roiling seas. Getting into the ocean-bound boat was difficult enough, but then we had to go four or five hundred tumultuous yards to the other ship. Once there I had to climb from my boat to the gangway of the other moving vessel. That was no easy task either! The ship's hull was bobbing up and down as much as seven to ten feet with every swell. The possibility of being crushed between my little boat and the side of that heaving vessel was constantly in my mind. One misstep would do it. I must have made the right steps because I'm here to tell the story. I made the passage between our vessels without being swept overboard, arriving drenched but whole.

Once there, the situation was still less than promising. The constant irregular movement of the sick bay was bound to make the operation much trickier than it would have been in a stable operating room on land. *All right*, I thought, *if it's necessary to save the poor man's life, it's worth a try.*

But when I examined the patient, in my opinion, there was nothing critical about his condition at the moment. I felt we could wait the coming twelve hours until we got to a real hospital back on land, rather than doing a risky procedure under less than ideal circumstances. I was reluctant to agree with the physician's decision. However, according to traditional medical protocol, as the doctor of record, he was in charge. My opinion was immediately over-ruled. He wanted to go right ahead and so he did.

The setting for that operation was far from ideal. The operating room on any ship is always in the center to avoid the radical movement of heavy seas. But that doesn't stop it from shifting. Under the conditions we were experiencing that day, any surgical procedure was bound to be dangerous. The anesthesia had to be spinal-type, one that, as any medical student knows, under adverse conditions could creep up his spinal cord, paralyzing him totally. If it reached his brain stem, it would be fatal.

We both knew the hazards involved, but I was the one of the two of us who was sweating where I stood by as, surgical tools in hand, he began the procedure. He went on; the appendectomy was done and, lo and behold, the appendix he removed turned out to be healthy and normal. Still, I could tell that the physician was pleased with himself, with the skill he had. He hadn't needed me there at all. That was clear.

I knew, and the general public should be aware, that even under the best of circumstances, an excellent surgeon doing lots of appendectomies will take out about ten percent of them that are normal and healthy. It isn't easy to tell from the symptoms how dangerous the situation is, and no doctor wants to take a life-threatening risk. The sailor on that ship hadn't needed his appendix removed, but ultimately for him it didn't matter. He had no complications and recovered normally. When we arrived back at the Naval base, he was able to walk down the gangplank on his own two legs.

And I was glad, after the operation, that I didn't have to repeat what was for me the most difficult part of the day. I didn't have to return to my ship over those rough seas. The exercises for all the ships were over and we were only twelve hours away from the base.

We were already heading back.

DOCTOR AND MISSIONARY

William Johnson

Life really began for me at age 17 when I was still in high school. It was then that I encountered what it was all about. Its purpose and meaning came to me through my brother, who was seven years my senior. I had had my struggles with him. Then he, an omnivorous reader who had been an atheist, came to know Jesus as his Lord and took on an entirely different—a positive—personality. He shared that experience of conversion with me in such a powerful way that I committed my life to Christ and to Christian service in every way that I could.

When I graduated from high school, I received a full scholarship to Columbia University's School of Journalism. Everything would have been paid for. I was highly tempted to take it, but I had a pull at my heart to be a doctor, thinking I could be of service to more people that way. So I turned down the scholarship.

Instead of Columbia, I went to Wheaton College, a private Christian college in Illinois, which had a highly regarded pre-med program. Having to pay my way through school, I worked 40 to 50 hours per week. In 1941 when World War II started during my freshman year, I was inducted into the U.S. Navy, but by the grace of God and the Navy, I was allowed to finish two years of pre-med at Wheaton before I went. Called to active duty in July of 1943, I was a Navy corpsman, cleaning more bed pans than I had ever known existed.

I had applied and been accepted by Northwestern University's School of Medicine in Chicago. When the dean realized that I had neither an undergraduate degree nor some of the prerequisite courses, I was called in to see him. After a lengthy discussion, he approved my entering medical school with a condition: I would take undergraduate courses at night while taking medical courses during the day. I willingly accepted his requirement. Adding to this full schedule, I had to attend Navy reserve classes and drills. I graduated from medical school in 1947 with a Bachelor of Science, as well as the M. D. degree. Later I earned a Masters in Experimental Medicine and Surgery. I had chosen surgery as my specialty, thinking that, if I ever did work overseas, I would be of greater help. By 1952 I had had four years of medical school and five years of surgical training.

The Korean War broke out in summer of 1950 and again I was inducted into the armed services, this time in the Army. I thought that I would get more surgical experience in the Army, although I could have chosen the Navy. Later, I often told my wife, Bobbie, that was a dumb choice for, in the Navy, one is considered both an officer and a gentleman, not just an officer. The Army sent me directly to a MASH (Mobile Army Surgical Hospital) in Korea. We were unloaded from a landing boat into cold, shallow water to wade ashore at Inchon, the harbor city for Seoul. It was December of 1952 and the weather was frigid. On shore there were no dry, clean uniforms waiting for us since we had not been expected at that time. We tried to warm ourselves by huddling around a bonfire, but were unable to sleep. After many hours a rickety old train with windows blown out took us inland to our post.

I was assigned to the 8076 MASH where emergency surgery treatment was performed a mile or two behind the front lines in north central Korea. It was the winter of 1952-53 and the severe weather caused many soldiers to lose arms and legs through frostbite. As quickly as was possible, the injured were flown by helicopter to our MASH where we operated on the most severely injured, who then were taken by ambulance to an advanced medical facility in the rear. The less seriously injured were patched up so that they could return to their units. With the temperature as low as minus 20 degrees, we operated on men who were almost frozen, which was probably the only reason they survived. We did our surgery in canvas tents heated by gasoline-fired potbellied stoves. The wind blew and the snow came in. There was no way to keep a totally sterile environment but it was likely, as I said, that the cold helped to keep them alive. Since there were frequent attacks on our MASH, our commanding officer insisted each one of us carry a Colt-45 at our hip inside our sleeping bag. I was afraid I was going to shoot my foot off rather than protect myself from the North Koreans.

The Army had only two highly trained surgeons in the Far East where the service was in desperate need of more. One day the colonel came in after I finished operating. He said, "Johnson, I got a telegram from Washington and it says that you can go to Philadelphia and take the exam to become a board surgeon. If you want to go, a small plane takes off in ten minutes. You'll have 30-days' leave." I said "Yes, SIR!" and packed in nine and a half minutes.

On the way, while in Tokyo awaiting a ride to the States, I called a medical school friend in Chicago who was the chief pathologist for the 4,000-bed Cook County hospital. It was in his area of knowledge that I needed to brush up on for the exam. He asked me,

"Where are you?" and I told him "Tokyo. I am on my way to take my orals which includes pathology and I haven't any way to study for it." He replied, "I'll meet you at Cook County morgue tomorrow if you can get there and spend the day with you." I got there and he coached me with lab work all day. Bobbie, who would become my wife (though she didn't know it then), was teaching at Wheaten Academy. She came to join me at the morgue and I pulled the cooling trays out to see how she tolerated corpses. She passed the test beautifully.

Later that month, I was notified that I had passed the orals to become a Diplomate of the American Board of Surgery. With this certification, I was assigned to a large Army hospital in northern Japan and was made chief of surgery.

During my 30-day leave, Bobbie and I decided to get married. We did, but she couldn't travel to Japan for two months. No military facilities for married couples were available in Sendai, so before she could come I had to pound the streets, knocking on doors, talking in a stumbling way to Japanese owners to ask one to rent a room to us.

Finally, I met a man who owned a rice paddy and agreed to build a house on it for us to rent. That home was built in 30 days! Since its foundation was balanced on a large boulder supporting the main beam under the house, it wiggled and wobbled. But even with frequent earthquakes the house stayed together. Still, it was a cold experience. As we slept at night, the wind howled and the snow came in onto our *tatami* mats. We awakened in the morning with snow on the mats and could see big cracks in the walls of the very fresh cherry wood used to build the house. We used two-inch adhesive tape to close the gaps, creating a crisscross pattern.

The owner came by the first month to collect the rent, asking Bobbie, "Where are your children?" She answered, "There aren't any" and he went away, disappointed. During the third month, still not satisfied, he handed us a Japanese box as a gift. We opened it up to find a ceramic Japanese god of fertility. At a later visit, when he came for the rent, he went away a very happy man for he learned that our first child was on the way. He must have thought that his gift gave us success.

We had a wonderful first year. Bobbie learned to cook over a charcoal hibachi and we learned how to survive in the inclement weather. We got a hospital bed to sleep on. They are narrower than twin beds so there was a lot of closeness.

When my tour of duty was completed, I was discharged in Indianapolis, our home city. We stayed there until the first of four daughters, Kathy, was born. She was always a little disappointed she hadn't been born in Japan, since she would have had a Japanese passport, as well as an American one. At the nearby Army hospital, one doctor in the obstetrics and gynecology department took care of Bobbie very well. They kindly let us stay on a few weeks after my discharge to allow Bobbie to deliver there.

When we left Indianapolis, I had one suit and Bobbie, two dresses. The back of the car was piled with diapers and baby. A surgical professor in Chicago had pleaded with me to come, join his practice, and be his partner. I would have had a ready-made practice with income. Bingo! But Bobbie and I had seen just a little bit of California and we told him we could not decide until seeing more of that beautiful state. Before that, however, I handled his practice for him for a month while he went on vacation.

Then we drove to California, toured around, and loved it. I called my professor friend and told him, "If I've left anything there, please ship it. We have to stay." So we started off with 25 or 30 dollars left to buy gas and 19-cent hamburgers, heading for San José. At that time there were two medical offices to rent and we chose one. We learned that the telephone directory was to be printed the next day. We had to get our number in it, thinking that was important for a new surgeon in town. We went to the telephone company with 30 minutes to spare and told them where I would be, even though I had not rented it as yet. Then we went back to the pharmacy where I had argued with the pharmacist over the rental price. He owned the building with offices above his shop and had a big smile on his face when he told me that he knew where I was going to work. I replied, "You do?"

"Yes," he said. "Welcome aboard. Your office is upstairs." It was on the second floor at such-and-such a suite and at the price that I had wanted. My question was "How did you know that I was going to take it?" He said, "The telephone company just called asking for your suite number."

I started medical practice knowing no one and without any patients. Every night I went to the emergency rooms of the two hospitals in San José. Usually, an accident had occurred. I would stitch up whoever was there and at times some became my patients. This way, plus referrals from doctors, I was able to begin my practice which, by the grace of the Lord, became successful. Often I worked 18 to 20 hours a day. Bobbie was my nurse, receptionist, and bookkeeper. When a patient came in, sometimes our baby could be heard crying in the back room.

During that time I became president of the national Christian Medical Society that emphasized short-term missions that lasted from a few weeks to a few years. (Long-term ones were for life.) Bobbie and I looked at each other. Since we were urging other Christian doctors to volunteer for mission work, we thought that we had better go ourselves. When help was wanted, needy countries knew to look for it from America. Our first mission trip was to Bolivia in 1962. When I left my solo practice in San José, I was scared to death that no patients would be there on my return. But referrals by doctors picked up when I re-opened my office and former patients returned, keeping my practice intact for another year.

Besides Bolivia, a few of the other short-term mission trips we took were to Thailand, Rhodesia, Swaziland, Comoro Islands in the Indian Ocean, Ecuador, Honduras, Guatemala, Philippines, China, and Belize. Conditions were primitive, including poor sanitation. For instance, Comoro Islands' only hospital had no window screens, allowing lots of flies inside. The nurses emptied bedpans out the windows where the contents were left until the next rainstorm washed them away through the lava. The stench was indescribable.

My first somewhat longer-term mission was to Kenya for one year with my family, during parts of 1970 and 1971. We had prepared our four daughters for bare living conditions, so when they opened the door to their new cement block home, they were pleasantly surprised. They attended a large missionary school along with children from many countries. There was a time when a box came to us marked "Obsolete. For Missionary Use Only." It contained surgical instruments which had gone through a fire and the chrome had burned off. They were junk and of no possible use in our work, so we trashed them. We had a few chuckles over this and were glad the sender was from a country other than the USA.

A second mission trip to Kenya was from 1975 to 1976. Our hearts were touched by the Kenyans for whom we would witness and hold chapel services, as well as tend to their medical needs. Bobbie, who earlier had her nursing training on the job, was more valuable than ever in assisting my medical work and, when our youngest was in junior high school, she went to San José City College and became a professional RN (Registered Nurse.)

By 1991 our daughters were grown and had left home. Bobbie and I had time to consider new opportunities. That September a total stranger called me about the desperate needs in Albania, the most backward country in the Eastern European bloc. The people there had suffered under a Communist regime for decades until President Hoxha had died and a democratic government was in place. The caller knew that the Albanian medical community was seeking help and we were invited for a tour of the country's facilities and practices. The capital, Tirana, had one hospital whose medical procedures were equal to those existing in the 1930s in the United States, and conditions in the countryside were even worse.

Medical school training was by professors reading to the students from the one book the school had for each course. The students themselves were given no interaction with each other or the staff, no hands-on experience. That has since changed with our visiting doctors holding country-wide conferences in Tirana for Albanian doctors to teach them the latest in surgery and other specialties. When we arrived, we brought medical books to them and created the first professional library. One doctor, reading one of the books, couldn't believe that the book didn't have the usual Communist propaganda in it.

When walking in the hospital or on the streets, we would be stopped by the Albanians asking in broken English, "Do you speak English? Are you Americans? Are you Christians? What is the Bible?" They would have been thrown into jail just by mentioning God if the Communists had still ruled the country. Their lives had been without spiritual content or hope. Our interpreters, all medical students, were sharp. One by one they came to Christ and wanted "to tell the world."

The doctors were very grateful for our coming and begged us to return next year. That we did, bringing a medical team. Some years after that there would be three such teams teaching modern medicine. Today the quality of medicine continues to improve. One team would meet with doctors from rural areas which I characterized as "medically disadvantaged" to teach them hands-on surgical techniques and medical practices.

These mission trips improved the lives of the Albanian people and gave them an opportunity to learn about our Christian faith. At the end of the first trip in 1991, I wanted to bring the doctors and nurses into a social atmosphere since, as a consequence of Communist rule, they had not interacted at all with one another. The best hotel in Tirana could provide only a dinner of cheese, bread, awful wine and greasy sausage. But it was a wonderful farewell party which brought them to talk openly with one another. I had brought 90 Bibles with me, and at the end of the evening I told them that the Bibles were on the table by the exit door and to help themselves. They did, some coming back a second or third time, wanting one for a relative. All the Bibles were taken. That was something I rejoiced over. Over a span of 15 years I flew to Albania 28 times to be with these fine people.

At first I thought the Albanian mission trips would only last three to five years. Word got around the American Christian medical community of volunteers, who joined us in such numbers, that the Albanian Health Fund was started. This organization was a means for them to coordinate their work schedules and contribute tax-deductible monies for mission expenses.

My last trip to Albania was in 2004. The organization is still thriving and continues its valuable work. I stepped down as president of the fund a few years ago, assuming the title of President Emeritus. The fund does not accept government help and relies on individuals, churches, and other organizations. Each doctor pays his own way completely. Our church, Saratoga Federated Church, today remains a valued sponsor.

Some years ago a close friend who founded Youth With A Mission called about a mission trip. YWAM had brought its message to every land in the world except one. He asked if we would go there. Bobbie and I tried to guess its name, but were not successful. It was Pitcairn Island in the South Pacific where, it turned out, the people are self-governing but under the sovereignty of Great Britain. The population is very small and has few visitors. We flew to Tahiti and from there a YWAM ship took us near Pitcairn Island where we were off-loaded onto a small boat sent to meet us. We found the medical conditions there deplorable and the people badly needing our attention. A rectangular, plain kitchen table was what we operated on. One day a man, about 90, came in doubled up because of a humongous hernia. I was successful in relocating the hernia back into his abdominal cavity and, with the help of Bobbie holding the hernia in place, I stitched him up.

While we were there, we operated on both the great-great-grandson, and the great-great-great-grandson of Fletcher Christian, the protagonist of *Mutiny on the Bounty.*

Over the years I have made some 70 mission trips, many times with Bobbie. My life and hers have been fulfilled by serving our Lord through witness and service to many people of this world.

A SLICE OF POST-WAR HISTORY

Larry Hawkinson

In the spring of 1946, while on the China Station after World War II, the USS MADDOX DDY31 spent much of her time supporting United States' interests in the struggle between the Nationalist Chinese under Chiang Kai Shek and the emerging Communist Power under Mao Tse Tung. She spent time with the larger American fleet in the area, but usually she operated in and out of Shanghai and Tsingtao, as well as making escorting runs to other areas such as Tiensien (at Taku), China and Jinsen (Inchon) in Korea. Many times we were involved in holding off skirmishes between the two Chinese factions. Indeed, on a few occasions the Communist and Nationalist small ships fired gun rounds and rockets back and forth at night, rounds that passed over our ship and others in Tsingtao port.

I was involved in one of the many minor experiences during that time. Our ship's whaleboat had been involved in an unfortunate collision with a sampan on the Huangpu River at Shanghai. It needed some repairs and Captain Santmayer felt it would be more prudent and less expensive to have them done locally, rather than through formal navel ship repair facilities. As the current JOPA (Junior Officer Present Afloat, an acronym based on SOPA for the Senior Officer), I was notified that the Captain wanted to see me.

Oh-oh, what have I done now? I thought, but in fact he gave me an interesting assignment.

The captain had remembered from his time in the area before the war that there was a local boat repair yard quite a way upriver. He felt that we could get the repairs done there with high quality and a reasonable price. When he had been there, the boatyard had been owned and run by an old Scotsman and his sons. The captain drew me a rough map showing me how to find the place and giving me the name of the yard. I was to take the boat and crew, as well as an LCVP (an amphibious craft assigned to our ship while in port) and its crew to return if the trip was a success. That was a challenging task which I set out enthusiastically to do.

The Huangpu River was very swift, as all of us who have been on it could attest. Upriver from Shanghai in those days the shore was a jumble of ruined or hastily rebuilt wharves, piers, warehouses, and other buildings.

Referring to the captain's map, I was certain that many of the boatyards we encountered looked promising even though no one in our party could read the Chinese markings on them. We stopped at each likely yard and attempted through pidgin Chinese-English to ascertain if the place was owned and run by the Scotsman the Captain had remembered. When asked if anyone spoke English, the typical response was negative or resulted in the English "expert" being pushed forward only to respond with his entire knowledge of English: "Hi, Joe!"

Eventually we located what had to be the right place and there I was introduced to the owner. My biggest disappointment of the day came when I realized that I could hardly understand his very heavy Scottish brogue. It had been modified with Chinese overtones dating from at least the early 1920s. Luckily his Chinese foreman spoke a version of English which I could just make out. Part of what I learned that day was that the Scotsman had been interned by the Japanese along with his four sons. They were all then to be sent to the South Pacific islands to be used as forced laborers, he on one ship and they on another. During the trip the Japanese convoy was attacked by American ships. His own vessel escaped attack, but he saw the second transport with his sons aboard sent to the bottom of the sea.

After the war he managed to return, reclaim his boatyard, and set it up in business again.

Although they used very primitive tools and techniques by our standards, the work done by the artisans there was of a very high quality. It was quite clear that our boat would be custom-repaired and, to say the least, in good hands. After evaluating other work at the yard and receiving an estimate of the cost of the repair needed, I decided both quality and cost were within the captain's guidelines, left the boat there, and returned to the ship with the LCVP and its crew.

In order to be certain that the boat was being well taken care of and attended to in a timely manner, I was required every few days to check out a jeep from the motor pool and return to the boatyard. The foreman had drawn me a map to show how to get there by road. Unfortunately, on the first trip back there I found myself hopelessly lost. The streets and roads in those days were almost devoid of vehicles but jammed with people walking and pushing carts. There were corpses of animals and humans everywhere. For me, it was truly an introduction to what we now call the "third world" level of living in both its poverty and lack of sanitation. I had been warned not to bother with checking the brakes on the jeep but to be sure that the horn was in good working condition. Indeed, if it weren't for that horn, I probably would never have been able to force my way through the throngs of people on the roads. Eventually I realized that I had no choice but to head for the river and then backtrack to whatever road looked like it would help in my upriver quest.

Aha! Suddenly I came on a formal, very military-looking, installation with masses of barbed wire, guarded gates, towers, warehouses, and the like. Surely I could find help there. However, when I attempted to approach the gates I was not too politely fended off by guards with drawn bayonets on their rifles. I did my best to convey to them my official duty and status, as well as my need for directions. I thought I looked impressive in my Navy uniform and I was driving an official U. S. Jeep. All that was to no avail. After some rather serious shouts which I easily interpreted as threats, I realized that it was useless to continue any further toward the river, retreated inland, and eventually stumbled upriver to my target destination. The boat was indeed repaired and repainted with a high level of expertise and, on a subsequent trip by LCVP, my boat crew and I were welcomed back to the ship.

What came of the well-guarded installation I had stumbled into on my jeep trip upriver in 1946? In the late 1940s I was watching a television news program at home in the States. There on the screen I recognized the fortified enclosure. According to the news story, the Nationalist Chinese forces had realized they could not hold their mainland enclaves any longer. They removed their huge cache of weapons, vehicles, supplies, and ammunition from their last mainland territory, along with precious hand-made artifacts, and sent them to Taiwan where Chiang set up his new government and built an historic museum.

That was quite a belated finish to my first interesting off-ship assignment as a new

Ensign in the United States Navy.

A TUMULTUS TIME:

ENDING SEGREGATION IN SCHOOLS

Richard Gousha

In 1954, the year of the Topeka, Kansas *Brown vs. Board of Education* unanimous decision, the Supreme Court ruled that racial segregation in public schools violated the Constitution of the United States. It was a consolidated opinion dealing with the cases involving Delaware, Kansas, South Carolina, and Virginia. Past decisions on whether segregation in the public schools deprived the plaintiffs of equal protection of the laws had been based on transportation rulings, not education. (For example, *Plessy vs. Ferguson*, 1896).

At that time, I was a 30-year-old Superintendent of Schools in Woodville, Ohio. During the following nine years I held several other jobs and completed my doctorate at Indiana University. In October of 1963, I was working as Superintendent of Schools at Cuyahoga Falls, Ohio when I was visited by the president of the Board of Education in Topeka, Kansas to find out whether I was interested in assuming the leadership of their school system. That was when I was informed that I was being considered as one of the candidates for the position of Delaware State Superintendent of Public Instruction, although I had filled out no application forms for the job. A screening committee of three professors (H. Thomas James, William Odell, both from Stanford University and Roy Hall, University of Delaware) had reviewed the records from a field of 50 educators and recommended six, among whom I was one, to the Delaware State Board of Education.

On November 6, I sent a telegram of acceptance to J. O. Small in which I said that I would be pleased to accept the offer I had received for the position effective on the first of January. At that time certain powerful political voices heard in the state belonged to Walter Hoey and Curtis W. Steen. Hoey was a Democratic state senator who was chairman of the General Assembly Joint Finance Committee, as well as chairman of the Senate Investigating Committee. Steen, also a Democrat, was from Dagsboro in southern Delaware and was senate president *pro tem.* A group of reporters heard Hoey expressing his disapproval of my appointment: "I understand he's a job-hopper. I don't think he's the man Delaware ought to have. A southerner was more qualified. A Delaware educator should have been selected for the job."

So from the start my selection was clouded in controversy.

During interviews with the State Board, all applicants, including myself, had favored the elimination of Negro school districts. In a telephone interview I had reiterated my philosophy on segregation. I said that for me, "The major question is not should there be integrated schools. I think we are beyond that. The problem is how segregated schools can be brought into the overall system in the easiest way."

However, at a blue-ribbon luncheon where neither of these critics were present, Governor Elbert Carvel offered kind words and, in his welcoming remarks, added that I did not have horns, did not have a forked tail, and wasn't cloven hoofed! "Dr. Gousha is not as much a stranger as you might believe. He once lived within three or four miles of where I lived in Baltimore, and it's always been perfectly respectable to come from Maryland."

In Delaware at that time 80% of all educational operating costs was controlled by the State Department of Public Instruction; 20% was raised locally. For construction, 60% of funding was done by the state; 40% was done locally. All transportation costs went through my office. At that time there were two transportations systems, one for black children and one for white. Separate companies, who bid for their contracts, ran them. There was a lot for me to find out about.

I remember, very soon after my arrival, driving with J. O. Small down the Du Pont highway. He was driving and about half-way down the state, south of Wilmington in Smyrna, he slowed down. "Dick," he said, "here's the problem in a nutshell." He was pointing to a little elementary school building next to another with a very different appearance. I could see the difference from the road. "There it is! There it is!"

In addition to getting acquainted with people all over the state, one of my major initial responsibilities was to study and revise the state education budget for the year 1964 and prepare to present it to the joint Finance Committee that Senator Hoey, who was a strong segregationist, chaired. Midway though the presentation he called a recess. From where I stood in front of his desk, I could see a machete he had displayed behind it. I felt threatened. When he spoke, it was worse, "Get off the desegregation issue or we'll have your ass! Do you understand?"

And I replied, "Senator, I work for the State Board of Education and they have instructed me to do away with the dual system of public schools. I will make every effort to do that!" He understood me and he didn't like what he had heard.

Shortly after this happened, my wife, returning from a shopping trip, stopped by a newsstand to pick up *The Delaware State News* with its headline: **WHO WILL PAY**

GOUSHA'S SALARY? That was a surprise to both of us, to say the least. I had a family to feed. Besides my wife, there were two children: Cathy, eleven, and Michael, eight years old. My pay was a line item and Senator Hoey had removed it from the budget. What came next? I was called by Governor Carvel to meet with him and Senator Hoey in his office where he told Hoey to put my salary back in the budget. He refused. Again, Carvel told him to do it. He refused again. Nevertheless, it was restored through the governor's budget and later even increased by the new Governor Charles Terry.

Just prior to my arrival as a consultant toward the end of 1963, the State Board of Education in a bill then in the General Assembly (House Bill 20) had proposed the merger of Middletown districts, both black and white. A Negro group expressed concern that the proposed plan would result in continued racial segregation: "We are not for a glorious state board-sponsored setup of continued segregation under the disguise of economy." Needless to say, the legislation did not go through.

At the same time Louis L. Redding, a black attorney representing the plaintiffs in the Delaware desegregation case (*Evan vs. Buchanan*), was quoted as saying, "The principal barrier we have in this state today to complete public school integration is the lethargy, the apathy, the indifference of the Negroes who would be benefited in taking advantage of the opportunity that is legally theirs." Unfortunately, his was one of the many observations that I encountered when I arrived. Later, the same lawyer cynically charged that segregation would influence legislation in the State Board's request for over 35 million dollars for Negro schools.

By the fall of 1963 a report initiated by the State Board with an appropriation from the General Assembly contained recommendations aimed at creating a more efficient administration of the Delaware school system. I later used a number of these in making needed changes.

When I arrived in the state, *Plessy vs. Ferguson (*separate but equal education) was in full effect. The Delaware Constitution and school law provided for three separate schooling areas: Negro, white, and Moor (a group of Moors had immigrated to the state from North Africa) with Indians from the Nanticoke tribe. (In 1744 a significant number of these Indians had moved eastward into Delaware from Maryland.)

A history of education in Delaware records that in 1869 the city of Wilmington had established the Howard school as the first elementary school in the state. In 1926 A. Pierre S. du Pont personally financed the construction of 86 school buildings for Negro pupils. Those one, two, and three-room frame buildings, heated by pot belly stoves, were still being used in 1963 and when an example of their condition came to light it was dismaying. Those who inspected them had found poor restroom ventilation and a need for more fencing. Structurally these building were on their last legs. These findings were typical of the black schools and in considerable contrast with the white ones.

As a result of a 1948 survey focused on Negro education, the legislature had voted to construct high schools for Negroes. Two years later one for each county had been completed: the Louis L. Redding for New Castle, William Henry for Kent, and William Jason for Sussex. Thus, in contrast to many inadequate elementary schools, there were three relatively new high schools in the state. The future usage of these schools still needed to be determined.

Following the 1954 Supreme Court decision, the final result of six years of maneuvering through the courts, the Delaware State Board developed a plan for integrating the Negro and white pupils at the rate of one grade a year. Negro pupils could choose to attend an integrated school, but simultaneously all Negro schools were allowed to continue in existence until some future legislation could be enacted to overhaul the system. By 1961 the U. S. District Court had set aside the grade-a-year plan on the basis that it would not accomplish integration rapidly enough. Delaware was exceptional. Nowhere, except in that state, did the courts order statewide integration, either immediate or gradual.

Taking advantage of free choice was not easy, even if the children of Negroes who opted to enroll in white schools were given transportation. If they wanted to enroll in the regular district, they could do that, by state board directive. What happened was that this directive was not very successful downstate. There were many blacks working in the poultry industry. If they wanted to send their youngsters to the regular district school, they could sign up. When the schools opened in the fall, someone where they worked went by and told them, "Sam, we think you're a good worker. We like the work you're doing. But we see that you've signed your child to attend (a particular school). We'd hate to see you leave." It was a powerful threat, guaranteed to keep the Negroes in their place and, as a result, only a small percentage of them was integrated under the free choice system.

When the public school system was reorganized in 1919 and 1921, the legislature had eliminated the separate tax on Negro property and appropriated funds for Negro schools. When I came to Delaware I found that, if a Negro family sent children to a Negro school, it was still not billed for taxes. When the same family later decided to send their children to a white school, the family got a tax bill.

After taking office in early January of 1964, I made my first visit to Sussex County where I was pretty much branded "down-state." I had an office in Wilmington, but my main office was in Dover. I remember driving down in my Oldsmobile with the radio on, listening to the talk shows' call-ins labeling me a Communist, "out of state," and everything else, including "catbird"--a slang term for a bird taking over, one that was given to feeding and caring for baby chicks of another kind who don't belong to it. Those were interesting times. Although that was where the greatest opposition to my appointment had been, I received a traditional warm welcome. During that visit I was subject to the usual joshing over the fact that I was an outlander and my selection over a native specimen aroused considerable controversy.

That month I spoke at the annual meeting of the Delaware School Board Association and afterwards was cheered in a standing ovation from members attending from throughout the state. In my speech I had said that I was "ashamed to be a part of the state's inadequate program for the education of Negroes. A dual system is an extravagance that the state can no longer afford. I will make every effort to abolish it at the earliest time possible."

By the middle of January a committee of representatives from the Department of Public Instruction, University of Delaware at Delaware State College (a Negro school), the Association for School Administrations, and State School Boards had been formed to address a number of issues. One was a complaint by the president of Delaware State, Dr. Mishoe, who noted the reluctance of school districts to accept his student teachers.

With the passage of the Civil Rights Act in February, integration was required for the transmission of federal funds. That legislation was an essential tool for integration because it provided machinery with which the judicial mandates were to be implemented. (It was not until July that President Johnson invited educational leaders to the White House to discuss the implementation of the Act.)

That same month a State Board of Education committee began a study of the future use of William Jason High School as a community college. On April 2 the National Association for the Advancement of Colored People Committee for Fair Practice Delaware Leadership Council formed a subcommittee to work immediately toward elimination of the *de facto* segregation in the Wilmington schools. At the State Board meeting Harry Zutz asked me, with the assistance of the joint committee of civil rights groups, to prepare a report on *de facto* segregation. It would be due on May 1, 1964.

On the first of January of 1965 Sussex County officials met with newly elected Governor Terry to ask for his intercession with the federal government. Twenty School Board members and administrators representing a dozen districts voiced objection to having federal attorneys tell them how to re-organize. They wanted to have freedom of choice extended.

The following month, on the ninth of February, an historical resolution acted to end the segregation of races in the public schools by voluntary agreement on the part of the School Boards of the Negro districts to dissolve and close their schools. At the same time School Boards of the neighboring white districts voluntarily agreed to accept pupils from the closed districts. A timetable in the resolution provided for the closing of 16 all-

Negro schools in 1965, six more in 1966, one in 1967, and the last, Jason at Georgetown, in 1970.

On February 25, in an amendment to the resolution of the ninth, the Board ordered three Negro schools in Sussex County closed on or before June 30, 1966 and the closing of Jason High School on the same date.

After a meeting with Governor Terry and the school officials involved, I announced that the "State Board will use all authority to ensure jobs for teachers affected by the closing of the Negro school system." The Governor expressed his approval and said that he would do all he could to cooperate. But early in February, Board members of the Negro Henry and Jason High Schools had opposed their closing, complaining that they had not been involved in the discussion about it.

On March 2 in Georgetown, a meeting was called to allow state school officials to explain their plans to Sussex County educators. This resulted in a heated discussion when I was told by the President of the Lord Baltimore School District that one of us was a liar. At the end of the meeting a motion to have attendees stand to demonstrate that the results of the meeting were not satisfactory to them was ruled out. Many of those there felt that there had been sufficient clarification of what was going on.

Late in April, a Democratic Negro Senator, Herman Holloway, harshly criticized members of the General Assembly and downstate Negroes for attempting to block the phase-out of the Negro schools. Representative Eskridge from Seaford and 17 members from southern Delaware had sponsored HB 175 which stated that "No public school shall be closed, phased out or otherwise eliminated except by an act of the General Assembly, provisions of the Delaware code to the contrary not withstanding." The effort to pass the measure was not successful.

But that month a bill that would give unemployed, qualified teachers first crack at faculty vacancies was introduced in the House of Representatives by its two Negro members. Its purpose was to assure jobs for teachers left without them by the scheduled phase-out of Negro schools systems. But Bill 185 died in committee.

Early in May, Commissioner of Education Francis Keppel, in a broad policy statement, set June 30 as a deadline for local school districts to file statements that they were in compliance with the Civil Rights Act of 1964. Since the Delaware situation was unique because all districts were under a federal court order to desegregate, I reported to the State Board and all local districts that the Board's resolution aimed at total desegregation by 1967 was not quite adequate to meet the policy of the U. S. Office of Education. Each school district would have to file a plan of acceptance. By June 4 the State Board of Education statement of compliance with the Civil Rights Law had been accepted.

That month Delaware State College officials announced that they had no particular problems that year in placing their graduating Negro teachers. They noticed a marked difference from the year before when they had felt a degree of reluctance on the part of downstate Delaware schools.

In June of 1965 the State Board of Education had strongly requested school districts receiving pupils from previously all-Negro schools to hire teachers displaced by the closing of those schools. They were asked to provide employment for teachers from Negro school districts in direct proportion to the number of Negro pupils received and in accord with the unit plan for the assignment of teachers. That request was not adequately implemented, and in February of the next year the State Board achieved the dissolution of the dual system in regard to the placement of teachers and issuance of certificates. However, one Board member opposed the policy and the largest downstate newspaper, in an editorial, stated that "The State Board is acting in a pretty high-handed and dictatorial fashion."

Following this State Board action, the President of the Board of Education of the Georgetown Special School District in a meeting to finalize integration plans, charged that I was a "power-hungry administrator employing goon tactics that violate our rights as a Board." He felt that the recent State Board resolution ordering local units to give priority to the hiring of phased-out Negro teachers had made the local Board members figureheads. Other participants called the ruling, "forcing them to become puppets of the federal government." In spite of these objections, they voted to desegregate.

Early in May of 1966 the Senate overrode the Joint Finance Committee and approved substantial raises for several state official, including myself. Senator Walter Hoey, chairman of the Finance Committee, was one of the three senators absent on the roll call. He did not wish to be involved.

By December of that year the National Education Association reported no displacement of teachers in Delaware. Addressing the state's efforts at integrating and desegregating schools, the association stated that Delaware had provided practices worthy of emulation by other states in dealing with pupil- and teacher-integration. The state's last all-black school was closed in 1967. All the Negro high schools had been phased out and 26 Negro schools closed. Some 307 Negro teachers had been transferred to school districts for white pupils, and 8,912 Negro pupils had been integrated into the white schools.

By 1968 desegregation in Delaware was a *fait accompli.* The state was the first of the southern and border ones with separated Negro and white educational systems to phase out the Negro schools and place all personnel.

Before I took the position of State Superintendent of Public Instruction for the state among a number of others, I had two specific goals. One was the integration of the separate Negro and white schools. Another was the consolidation of the 80 or so districts into 48 more efficient units. A draft of a proposed bill known as the Educational Advancement Act, when approved by the State Board, would reduce the number to approximately 20.

Two years after I left, in July of 1969, the General Assembly enacted this law. The Board was given jurisdiction to reorganize districts throughout Delaware with the specific exception of the Wilmington school district. The legislation also provided that consolidated district school systems should have enrollments between 12,000 and 19,000 students. Because Wilmington schools already enrolled more than 12,000 students, they were prevented from joining other districts, as were two other suburban districts, Newark and Alfred I. du Pont.

On January 3 of 1972 Louis Redding and Irving Morris, attorneys for the plaintiffs, in accordance with Federal Rules sought to modify this important Act, bringing to court additional plaintiffs and defendants in the *Brenda Evans, et al. Defendants vs. Madeline Buchanan, et al. Defendants.* The defendants were all the members of the State Board of Education.

The plaintiffs complained that the Act was designed to perpetuate a racially discriminatory school system. The drawing of the district lines circumscribed the overwhelmingly black Wilmington area into an identifiable black school district. It re-established the state-mandated pattern of segregated schools in New Castle County. The legislature's reasoning for imposing a maximum size limitation was that larger districts might be administratively unmanageable. During the court proceedings, using it as an example, I testified that the Milwaukee School District (where I was then Superintendent of Schools) could be effectively administrated even though total enrollment was 125,000. The Court stated that, while 12,000 was rational, a substantially greater maximum size would also be rational.

The District Court found that the Educational Advancement Act did not purposefully foster discrimination but, nevertheless, it had a discriminating effect and that effect was a constitutional violation that could only be remedied by requiring mandatory busing for racial balance throughout the New Castle public schools. A massive school desegregation plan was imposed on New Castle County--one which, on April 28 of 1980, the U. S. Supreme Court left untouched. Over the dissent of three judges, the Court refused to review an order combining 11 independent districts to remedy segregation in one of them: Wilmington.

I had left Delaware to become Superintendent of Schools in Milwaukee, Wisconsin early in June of 1967 and much of this occurred after that. As I expected, following my resignation there was considerable sentiment for the Board to pick a local person for State Superintendent. But contrary to the way two Board members had felt when I first arrived, they said upon my leaving that "Gousha has done an outstanding job.

One argument for naming a local person now is that he has everything in pretty good order. When he was hired, we felt he would not be subject to local pressures in getting Delaware over the hump in school desegregation."

A local superintendent, one of the six final candidates in 1967, was then appointed.

MY FRIEND SASHA

Dorothy Horning

I've always been fascinated by wolves. As an avid dog lover, I considered the wolf to be a "super dog," the most beautiful and intelligent of them all. The more I read about wolves the more I admired their well-developed social structure. I pictured that boy being raised by wolves in a legend. And I related to Lois Criswell's book, *Arctic Wild,* about living with wolves in Alaska. While others dreamed of fame and fortune, I fantasized about being in the Arctic with those wolves, too.

This went on for many years. I even mused about having a wolf for a companion while my husband, Norm, and I went on enjoying dogs and cats. It was just a dream, an impossible dream, one that was completely out of keeping with the quiet residential neighborhood in suburban Ohio where we lived. But it persisted. At one time we had a dog who was supposed to be one-quarter wolf and we had several dogs named *Wolf.*

Then we moved to northern California. We had always wanted to live either in the woods or on a mountain and, in the village of Woodside, we found the perfect spot. We purchased three acres on a mountainside heavily forested with redwoods. The terrain was rugged, with a little mountain stream running down through it. We wanted to keep all of its natural beauty, so we left the forest floor of ivy and ferns untouched. From our property to the mountain top, all was wilderness.

There we built our dream house. It had somewhat the look of a chalet, with a very steep roof and decks which surrounded the house. The exterior walls were mostly glass, so wherever we were inside we could look out into the forest. Everywhere there were wild animals: deer, raccoons, skunks, opossums, an occasional coyote and mountain lion. With all those about, I thought to myself, *hmmmmmm...I wonder...*

I read more articles about having a wolf in the household. Without exception, everyone advised emphatically, "DON'T DO IT! Wolves are dangerous, ferocious animals. They cannot be domesticated. Don't ever bring one inside your house. A wolf cannot be housebroken and it will tear your sofa to shreds."

I treasured my sofa, but on the other hand I already knew that a wolf would kill only for food. It would never attack just for sport. Moreover, there had been no documented case of a healthy wolf ever attacking a human throughout all of North America. Wolves have been much maligned in literary writing. And no wolf ever really ate Little Red Riding Hood's grandmother! A wolf would fit into our family. I just knew it! It was a compelling, beautiful dream but, still, only a dream.

Then one Sunday morning Norm saw an ad in the paper: "WOLF CUBS FOR SALE!" Naturally we were curious, although, of course, we knew we would never consider buying one. There could be no harm in answering the ad, just to inquire. I flew to the telephone and talked to a Bob in the Grass Valley area who owned the pair of adult wolves who had produced the litter which he was offering for sale. I wrote down directions to his ranch. It was a lovely day and a drive farther north would make a nice excursion. We knew that we would just be looking.

We both felt very excited as we approached our destination. After all, we were about to see some real live wolves. After a long driveway leading to Bob's house, we arrived at the front yard. There they were: Bob with seven tiny wolves tumbling about him on the grass! The two feral parents were fine-looking, healthy gray timber wolves enclosed in a large pen. The babies looked much like German Shepherd puppies, but there was an indescribable difference about them—something exotic. We talked to Bob and played with the small creatures for a while. Our hearts just melted. From that moment on there was no turning back: we selected a spunky little female, closed the deal, and loaded her into the car for the ride home. We had our Sasha, only five weeks old!

Sasha slept in my lap during the trip back. As soon as we arrived home, we set her down on the deck to introduce her to the other animals. Our two dogs and both cats came running up, full of curiosity. Sasha rolled over onto her back in full submission. At first they just sniffed. Then they sniffed and sniffed some more. After that they sniffed again. Then they poked her gently with their paws, seeming to sense that there was something different about that animal. But they accepted her anyway, soon walking away.

As Sasha grew up, the five animals became great friends and formed a sort of pack. Even when she grew larger and stronger, the cats permitted her to pick them up by the scruffs of their necks and carry them around. During the day while we were at work, the young Sasha stayed with the dogs on the decks which surrounded the house. The cats, of course, could leap over the railings and run out into the forest. In the evening when we arrived home, we always got a royal greeting from all of them.

Not once was Sasha ever on a chain or in a cage. Whether in the house or out in the forest, she always ran free. As she grew up, she matured into a fine, healthy animal about the size of a large German Shepherd, with thick gray fur and flashing intelligent, yellow wolf eyes.

Sasha was as agile as a cat! Not only could she leap over the railings, but she could easily jump up and run along the narrow ones enclosing our decks. From there she was off the deck and away for a day in the forest. With a giant leap she could even get up onto the roof of the house. Once she was there, she loved to amble around. One day I watched as she lost her footing and slid down the steep pitch, narrowly missing a large jagged boulder when she landed.

She particularly liked to be on the roof during a storm, climbing up to the skylight at the very peak and peering down at us as we sat in the living room. The rain would be pelting down, but there she was! Norm was very excitable and he would start shouting, "She's going to fall through! She's going to fall through!" I myself just thought the situation humorous since I knew that she wouldn't step on the slippery glass of the skylight. *I don't believe this,* I thought to myself. *Here we are, two middle-aged people sitting in our living room minding our own business, and worrying that a wolf is going to come hurtling through the air down on top of us.*

Like our two dogs, Sasha had the run of the house when she wanted it. She was always well-behaved. I believe that the dogs trained her, somehow communicating what behavior was acceptable so that she emulated them. I never tried any "Come, sit, stay." regimen with Sasha. It seemed unwolflike and beneath her dignity. She slept in our bedroom, sometimes even on our bed. Not once did she leer toothsomely at my sofa.

Contrary to the dire warnings we had heard, Sasha was easily housebroken. There was one memorable occasion to the contrary, however, when she was still very small. I was going out the door on my way to work when I got a whiff of that smell which is the bane of every puppy owner. I was already running late, but I had to take care of this before I left. Taking a cursory look around the room, I failed to find anything. Then, with my nose downward, I did a thorough search. Still nothing… I stood upright and in that position it seemed that the smell was more noticeable. I directed my nose upward and, sure enough, the smell was stronger. It was coming from above, from the ceiling!

Standing there in utter bewilderment I suddenly had a clue: our living room had a very high cathedral ceiling, but all around the periphery of the room at the top of the vertical walls ran a soffit for holding indirect lighting. Sasha had apparently gone up the stairs into the loft at one end of the living room and squeezed her small self through onto the soffit. That gave her access to run all around the outside of the room at the ceiling level! *Why, that little dickens,* I thought to myself, as I went outside to bring our longest ladder to inspect the soffit. Sure enough, directly above the piano I found what I was looking for.

Sasha was always the gentlest of creatures, with a very sweet demeanor. On one occasion she even permitted me to pull food out of her mouth. When she approached us with a little cock of her head, wriggling her body, she was irresistible. She didn't bark or snarl or growl. The only time we ever heard her vocalize was when occasionally she would go up the mountain, sit there, and howl.

Except for Norm and me, Sasha would not go near another human being. When visitors came to our house, she would promptly depart, go out into the forest, climb up to a higher level, and sit there watching the house. Not until she knew the coast was clear would she return.

There was one occasion, though, when I suffered serious physical harm because of her. I had just come home from work, parked my car on the asphalt pavement at the lower level, and started up the concrete steps set into the hill leading up to the house. Suddenly Sasha appeared out of the woods and came bounding joyously toward me. With one final exuberant leap she landed squarely on me, her two front paws on my shoulders. Back I went, hurtling down the stairs backwards to the bottom where my head hit the pavement with a solid thud. Norm was standing on the deck above, watching in horror. He rushed down to scoop me up off the pavement and into the house. Fortunately, I had no broken bones and, except for a concussion, there was no lasting damage. Still, every fiber of my being was in agony and I was laid up for several weeks.

Our wolf loved games. In one of her favorites, I would sit in the living room and put a woolly stocking cap on my head. She would pretend not to notice but then, when I would least expect it, she would dash up, snatch the cap off my head and run pell-mell into another room where she waited silently for me to come to retrieve the cap. I came in, searching all over for her. When I finally found her and pretended to scold her severely, her eyes would twinkle and she would leap about in delight.

We never informed our neighbors that Sasha was a wolf. None of them ever saw her up close. Because they only caught glimpses of her darting through the woods or sitting on a knoll, watching, they probably just assumed that she was a dog. Once, when Norm and I, the two dogs and Sasha went walking through a field, two teenage girls came by on horseback. We heard one say to the other, "Hey, Judy, there's that dog that I saw yesterday and I thought it was a wolf! Can you imagine? I thought it was a wolf!" They both laughed as Norm and I walked on.

There were some occasions when Sasha was recognized as a wolf. She loved to ride in the car, a hatchback model. The back had a large window and people in cars behind ours could see her clearly. Several times, when we turned off the highway into a restaurant or gas station, the car behind us would follow us in and the people in it would ask, "Is that really a wolf in your car?" We had to admit that it was.

These were the happiest of times! Those Sasha years were among the best in my life. But, alas, they were only too brief.

One night, when Sasha was four years old, I was preparing for bed when she walked into the bedroom obviously in distress. She couldn't breathe. I could see that something was terribly wrong so I called Norm and we rushed her to the emergency veterinary clinic. After X-rays, the doctor told us that she must have received a violent blow to her chest, damaging and misaligning her heart and lungs. That was hard to believe because she had no visible marks on her body. Could she have been kicked by a horse or a deer? Or had she fallen off the roof again, this time landing on that treacherous rock? We would never know.

The next morning I picked her up and took her to our regular vet who told us that there was nothing he could do for her. We would just have to wait and see whether she would be able to adapt to these changes. I went to work. About two o'clock that afternoon Dr. Johnson called to say that Sasha had died.

My world crumbled. How could this be? Only yesterday Sasha was her happy, vivacious self, cavorting through the woods, delighting us with her antics, and in every way becoming dearer to us. Now my beautiful, beloved Sasha was gone forever… I would never, ever, see her again…

It was a long time before the raw, jagged edge started to wear off my grief for Sasha. My friends advised me to get another wolf. I never considered it. Some dreams are so special that, when they come true, they can only be lived once.

SIX TRAVEL VIN YETS

Tom McCollough

(1) The Jesus Boat

In 1867, Mark Twain and a small group of pilgrims arrived at the Sea of Galilee traveling on horseback from Capernaum to the north. Enthralled, they saw a boat under sail offshore and hailed the skipper in hopes of convincing him to give them a ride on the holy waters where Jesus walked two thousand years ago. The captain demanded $8 to take the group for a ride. By consensus, they decided that $8 was outrageous, and offered $3. The skipper immediately pulled away leaving the pilgrims disappointed and mad at the Palestinian infidel.

My wife, two surly teenage daughters, and I, 105 years later, were driving along the Sea of Galilee just below Tiberius. We had been told that, at a nearby kibbutz, the "Jesus Boat" would take tourists for a boat ride. We pulled into the parking lot, bought our tickets for $12 per person, and walked out on the pier to wait for the boat.

An hour later, we heard the motor and saw the Jesus boat approach. It was made of horizontal wood slats, sloping high off the water fore and aft. There were several masts, but no sails. From stem to stern it was 40 feet long, and 15 feet wide amidships. Benches lined the outside edges of the boat. In principle the boat was the same size and shape that Twain had hailed 100 years earlier.

A Japanese family had also arrived for our ride. Questioned by the crew as we boarded, we confessed that we were Americans. After being seated, we were startled to hear the Japanese national anthem being played over a very loud speaker, followed by The Star Spangled Banner. Then, with a great flourish, the Japanese and American flags were run up the masts. After pulling away from the dock, we were offered pop and snacks at an inflated price. For half an hour we headed north with the Golan Heights to our right, then turned about, and motored south for another half hour or so.

What might have been a thoughtful spiritual journey, ended being absurd, even silly. The present day was too much with us.

(2) Senator Hugh Scott

If you are over 50 years old, you might remember the name of Hugh Scott, the renowned Republican senator from Pennsylvania. Scott was deeply involved in the Watergate Affair. He was among the contingent who, after the tapes were discovered, famously went to Nixon to tell him to resign. After Scott left the Senate, he joined a liberal law firm as a lobbyist. (All Washington liberal law firms have a token conservative aboard.) We had hired a lawyer from his firm to help us with a Washington problem. That firm was proud of its famous conservative partner and made a point of introducing clients to him as part of burnishing all of its members' credentials.

"Let's have lunch with the senator in the Senate Dining Room," our lawyer proposed and so it was arranged. It was the first time I had ever been in the Senate Dining Room, and I must admit I was pleased to have the opportunity to rub shoulders with the senators. Our table for four was in the center of the room. I looked around to see if I could see any famous faces, but I didn't.

I knew from hearsay that one soup offered every day traditionally was the bean soup. I ordered it. I resolved to relax, sit back, and enjoy the luncheon. But I was a little concerned about what we might talk about. I didn't want to be either condescending or boring.

A recent issue of *Architectural Digest* had featured the Scott collection of Asian artifacts that he and his wife had put together during a lifetime of assignments and travel. I thought that subject would do for starters. The senator seemed pleased to tell us about where he and his wife had traveled and where particular pieces had been acquired. Over dessert and coffee the senator remarked, "See that table over there under the stained window? That's the table where every day during the Watergate hearings the key Republican leadership met for lunch. Last year a waiter discovered wads of chewing gum under the table, so it was taken out of commission to be cleaned. When the table was turned over, another discovery was made: the table had been bugged, we assume by Nixon. He must have known exactly what we were saying about him."

What a choice morsel to end the luncheon with!

On the way out at the *maitre d'* station I spotted a wicker basket filled with match books stamped with *Senate Dining Room*. I grabbed a handful as a memento of the lunch with Senator Scott. For years I left one of those match books on our coffee table at home when we had guests. No one has ever noticed or mentioned the match book. So much for hobnobbing with famous senators!

(3) Cuddly Dangers

Adventure is a word usually associated with big game hunting, bungee jumping, snake infested jungles, or trips to far away places. Occasionally my wife and I have had our own adventures. For example, we once rafted down the Colorado River and the rapids through the Grand Canyon.

But one adventure had a softer, more gentle feel about it. We traveled to Churchill in Manitoba, Canada, to see the polar bears before they went out on a frozen Hudson Bay for the winter. The perfect time to go to Churchill is on Halloween when the bears are migrating through the town on their way to the tundra to await the coming long cold. We arrived on October 29th when the temperatures were already below freezing and the winds blowing light snow sideways.

Churchill has one main street dominated by a few motels, restaurants, and apartment buildings. Side streets lead to some houses, churches, schools, a post office, a community center, and a few stores. Most of these frame buildings are not over one or two stories tall. The airport is located out of town, but a heliport and the railroad station are in the downtown area, too.

On the evening we arrived, we were bused to a staging center several miles from the tundra at the edge on the town. Groups of 15 tourists were transferred to "tundra buggies," contraptions that look like buses with small decks on the back and huge five-foot tires. We rumbled out on the tundra for a half-hour, arriving at a strange sight: a "train" of five buggies linked together where visitors could live for a few days among the bears. This peculiar train had a dormitory, kitchen, dining room, and a classroom/living room where passengers stayed during the daylight hours.

"We are sure to see bears tonight," said the guide. "They hang around this spot because they like the odor of the food and the antifreeze." Sure enough, when the spotlights were turned on, about eight polar bears were lounging around, looking relaxed and cute. The light didn't bother the animals while they gave us an amusing display of bear behavior. We saw two bears standing up, sparring. They seemed to be serious about fighting. Others pushed snow around with their noses, rolled over in the whiteness, or stood up against one of those huge tires as if begging for a handout.

We went to bed that first night in Churchill satisfied that our quest had already been fulfilled, and with the mistaken notion that polar bears really were the way they looked: cute, cuddly, and perhaps even kindly.

All of the next two days were spent out on the tundra looking for, and finding, bears. During that time we saw fifty or more of them. Lunch was served in the heated buses. When a group of bears was located, the driver would radio the others, and soon we were gathered on the spot, watching, until the bears wandered away. Little thrills were common. For example, the bears liked to come right up to the buggies, stand up on their hind legs, and look directly at us caged humans, inches away, nose to nose. They did not seem ferocious, but we were warned repeatedly not to put our arms outside the bus.

On our second night in Churchill, we had been driven to a nearby wood frame church for a lecture about the history of the town. After the talk, we put on our coats and gathered in the vestibule, expecting to return to the motel, when we heard the news.

"Sorry, but you can't leave. There is a bear on the front steps of the church. We've just called the animal control people."

In a few minutes we heard a pick-up truck arrive and several firecrackers go off. That was all it took. The bear left promptly. That day we learned that the best way to make a polar bear move is to make unpleasant noises like setting off firecrackers, firing a gun, or banging on pots.

I still think that polar bears are not dangerous. But then, when it is Halloween in Churchill, the little children go trick-or-treating with their fathers carrying shotguns. Perhaps they know more than I do. Hmm… If you were a hungry polar bear, what would you think of seeing a tot carrying a big bag of candy?

(4) St. Katarina

Our destination was St. Katarina, the ancient monastery in the desert at the foot of Mount Sinai where Moses descended with the ten commandments, and where he heard God speak to him from the burning bush. We had flown from Tel Aviv to Sharm el Sheikh at the northern tip of the Red Sea, landing at an airport consisting of a shack made of corrugated tin. At that time--in the early seventies--no welcoming hotels had been constructed.

Once there, we were loaded onto a desert bus, along with an armed guard, a doctor, food for a week and a guide who spoke mostly in French. After spending one night in an oil field barracks, we bumped through the hot, dusty Sinai desert on dry wadis and old camel trails until we arrived at the monastery late in the afternoon.

"Hurry," the guide said. "The sun is going down and I want you to see the burning bush before it's too dark."

The stone monastery walls were 30 feet high, surrounding a group of ancient buildings which included two churches, a dormitory gallery, and the famous library housing a world-class collection of religious icons, mosaics, books, and silver. When we were there, ten Benedictine monks in tennis shoes lived and would die as the guardians of the priceless treasure. After any one of them died, he would be buried until his flesh was gone. Then his bones were dug up, dismantled, and placed in the ossuary outside the main walls.

We crowded through the front gate and came to a short downward flight of steps with a painted sign in English: "To the Burning Bush." Huddling together on a patio at the foot of the stairs, we were directed to look at an urn with a plant in it. Most tourist groups have someone who is the bane of the excursion, a person who annoys with a loud mouth, inappropriate remarks, thoughtless actions, and rude manners. Our pariah was a 20-year-old man from Brooklyn who irritated us hourly. As we looked at the plant, we heard his sarcastic voice from the back of the crowd, "My God, it's a raspberry bush!"

About four o'clock the next morning in the cold and dark we were awakened to wash with cold water, dress, eat, and join a camel train. We were going to trek up Mount Sinai to visit the small chapel there and see the sunrise over the desert from that peak. I had a toothache and decided to remain below to wait for my wife and our two daughters to return at midday. My daughter, Elizabeth, was a shapely teenager and a beauty. We heard later that, on the ascent, she had offered her camel guide a cigarette. The Bedouin had immediately gone to our tour guide and offered 18 camels to buy her.

We didn't sell.

If it had been 21 camels, maybe…but that's another story.

(5) I Shot the Mayor of Haifa

A grant was awarded by Bank One and WBNS-TV in Columbus, Ohio to produce a one-hour film in Israel about the educational system there. The film's title was to be "Israel's Second Line of Defense." To produce any one-hour film requires at least nine hours of footage. To make sure we would have enough, we planned a ten-day shoot. I agreed to go to Tel Aviv a month in advance to scout locations, outline the script, and brief the participants. My advisor in Israel was to be Moshe Smilansky, a noted sociologist at the University of Tel Aviv, and a frequent consultant to the Israeli Minister of Education.

The Israeli education system was unique, often experimentally based on specific educational or commercial needs. For example, at one time bulldozer operators were in short supply, so a school to train drivers was opened. I witnessed 12–year–olds driving huge bulldozers, practicing pushing great mounds of earth around. Some children of Israeli immigrants came from undeveloped countries. I visited a residential school in Haifa where those students were being taught to use tableware for the first time in their lives. Babies and little children of "kibbutzniks" lived in independent co-ed dormitory/cottages so that their mothers and fathers could work outside the home every day. Many traditional basic-skills schools required that students tend a garden as part of everyday schooling. Israel was a rich source of ideas about inventive schooling and we were eager to bring those ideas to the States.

When I arrived in Tel Aviv, I wrote a ten-day shooting schedule and awaited the arrival of the film crew: a photographer, a sound man and a set-up man. Then the first call came that the crew would only be able to stay eight days. While I was rewriting our work plan, the second call came: they would only be able to stay three days. That made the job impossible. A one-hour film requires at least nine hours of usable footage. (On a good day of shooting there may be 15 minutes of editable footage, if you are lucky.) Even worse, when their plane arrived, there were only two, not three, people in the crew. No one ever explained to me why this had happened. If I had been wise and experienced, I would have cancelled the shoot on the spot and sent the crew home. But instead I forged ahead. The two-man crew had been drinking heavily on the plane trip and stumbled off with both jet lag and hangovers. They expected to go to a hotel to sleep themselves into better condition, but I dragged them to the first day's location. Bad vibes began immediately as I pleaded with them to make the most of the little time we had.

The next two days were intense. The two men were sullen; I was demanding. About once an hour they asked to be excused so that they could go wandering off to shoot some footage of normal life in Israel that could be used in the final film in transitions from one scene to another. I refused.

On the last day, before their plane left, we were scheduled to interview the Mayor of Haifa who permitted many educational innovations to take place in his school district. "No!" yelled the crew leader. "We won't go. We already have too many talking heads. Anyway, it's too far to drive."

That was the moment when Dr. Smilansky arrived. He had planned to go with us to Haifa to introduce me to the mayor. I explained that we were canceling the shoot and he roared, "You can't! I promised him. And if we don't go, he will never let me back into his school system." Feeling like a beaten dog, I looked at the crew chief.

"All right," the cameraman replied. "We will drive up to Haifa with one light and one camera with no film, and you can take a tape recorder. We'll fake the interview. Then drop us off at the airport."

So I shot the mayor of Haifa. The single light was set, the camera whirred, I turned on the tape recorder. The mayor seemed thrilled to answer my thoughtful questions. Needless to say, his words didn't make it to the cutting room floor. No footage was available to cut.

(6) At Sea in a Foreign Land

At the peak of political tensions, someone in my home office thought it might be a good idea if I visited the Minister of Health in Libya. I knew something about the repressive Kaddafi regime since his government had forbidden all American operations. Our Tripoli office had been closed and the entire staff fired. Still, I didn't question the wisdom of going there.

My company was curious to evaluate the country's Maternal and Child Heath operation. Absolutely no marketing or commerce was permitted there, although we knew large quantities of our products were being bought through surrogate countries.

I didn't speak a word of Arabic. So it was arranged that our Athens manager, who was Arabic-speaking, would precede me by two weeks to arrange transportation, hotels, and appointments with government officials. He would be my translator. Because I had recently been in Israel, it was necessary to disguise the fact by issuing me a new passport.

I flew to Tripoli from Rome. Before landing, the Alitalia flight crew passed out necessary arrival documents, but they were entirely in Arabic. I asked the hostess to help me, and she reassured me, "Don't worry. They won't be needed." When I walked out the Arrival passageway, a young soldier pointed a machine gun at me and waved me back. The other passengers were passing me by, and I hollered, "What does he want?" Someone hollered back, "Your landing documentation." I reached for my landing form. It was still all in Arabic. I screamed, "What does the first line say?"

"Your name."

Little by little, with help I was able to fill out the form. I handed it to the soldier who smiled and waved me on. I could see my business associate on the other side of passport control and in a few minutes I almost fell into his arms.

The drive to the hotel was memorable because we encountered a blinding sand storm. By then it was nightfall, so we rolled up the car windows and inched along in the dark. When we finally reached the derelict old hotel, the lobby teemed with a horde of shouting men trying to reach the front desk. My friend told me to wait and I watched him walk behind the desk, take a key from the rack, and return to escort me to my room. The temperature was at least 90 degrees and I was already wet through. The small bedroom had a single bed with some sheets, an open window without screens, and a tiny bathroom.

The shower head was in the middle of the bathroom ceiling between the toilet and the sink. There was no tub or shower stall and the floor drain was slimy with mold. Neither was there any air conditioning!

I took my coat and tie off and lay down in a pool of perspiration. In fifteen minutes I decided it was too hot to try to sleep, so I went to the lobby to see if I could get a cold drink. I knew that no alcohol was permitted, but I hoped for an ice-cold something. The lobby was filled with men of every kind: Japanese, Chinese, blond men (Germans or Scandinavians, I assumed), and assorted swarthy Middle Easterners. All of them were business men in Libya's favor. A television set was blaring a show about squirrels bouncing around among Western-looking trees. A small bar was serving orangeade, warm without ice.

My translator had explained that, in this culture, I should be circuitous in conversation. It was impolite for strangers to ask direct questions. (Try holding a conversation with strangers sometime without asking a question.) Through the entire first day of appointments I struggled with speech formulations. I began with, "I am interested in nutritional practices here in Libya, particularly pediatric practices." That was usually enough to start a conversation.

But I soon noted a pattern. As soon as we left an appointment in the Health Ministry or a hospital, a second group of two or three people would appear and want to know what we had just discussed. These were the political authorities checking on the government employees. Needless to say, I was never able to relax. The minister, as well as the doctors and nurses we met who had usually trained in England or the States, was knowledgeable and competent. (When Kaddafi took over, many professionals had fled to

Italy. He told them to return or he would arrest their families. They returned.) But the facilities and equipment I saw were third rate.

My visit lasted three days. On the last one I was taken to see the warehouses where government pharmaceuticals were stored. The outside temperature was about 100 degrees, so inside it must have been 150. The drugs were stored in corrugated sheds with dirt floors and no air conditioning. I held my tongue, but knew that they must be having serious problems. (Insulin, for example, must be refrigerated and never be exposed to temperatures over 72 degrees.)

On that last day in Libya, I thanked everyone for their hospitality and information. Feeling bold, I asked, "Is there any way I might help you?" "Yes," they told me. "Our storage facilities are outdated and need to be improved. Could you send information about modern storage systems?" I agreed to send all I could gather.

On the way to the airport we picked up a stranger and parked at a small, empty store front with its blinds drawn. After we entered the building, the door was locked. The stranger who was riding with us handed me a large box, telling me, "This is for you, to remind you of your visit here." I opened the box and there was a beautiful grey floor-length Arab gown with elaborate embroidery. He continued, "But you can't tell anyone you got it here or bought it here. Pack it with your dirty clothes, and let anyone who sees it assume you brought it with you."

The stranger left the vacant store alone and I asked, "What was that all about?" "He was a former employee who wanted to do you a favor so that you'd be beholden to him. If he ever needs a favor, you are obliged to respond."

The translator and I flew back to Athens without further incident. I was mush from those three tense days. We went directly to Piraeus, on the coast, for dinner. After I asked my friend to order for me, I slugged down two martinis on the rocks. When the first course arrived, it was a plate of tiny oysters on the half-shell, surrounded by lemon wedges. When I squeezed lemon juice on the oysters, they all squirted juice back at me and shriveled as if to avoid the dousing.

Thank God for cold gin.

MY KOREAN TOUR OF DUTY

Carl Szybalski

Little did I know when I enrolled for classes at the University of California at Berkeley in 1948 that I would end up fighting a war in Korea.

But prior to my Korean stint I had already served in the U. S. Army from December of 1944 to December 1946. As a corporal, I had served one and one-half years in the Philippine Islands until World War II ended. I had been part of a contingent designated to attack Japan if there were no surrender after the second atomic bomb was dropped. Fortunately for me, that surrender came.

In the early part of my term at Berkeley I thought that, if there were another war, I wouldn't want to serve as an enlisted man. So I thought that I would sign up at the Reserve Officer Training Corps (ROTC) which, if there were another war, would ensure me the rank of an officer. As I suspected would happen, in 1950 another war broke out on the Korean Peninsula. So when I graduated, after some training at Fort Meade, Maryland, I was called up to participate as an ordinance officer. That training had gone well, so I found myself on my way to Korea.

At that time, as a "Distinguished Military Graduate," I was offered the opportunity to join the regular Army, but I didn't do it.

My trip on the ship west was very different from my previous Army experience since officers eat well in nice dining rooms and sleep well in spacious bedrooms. We were about two weeks at sea before we landed at Inchon where, later on, General MacArthur invaded. In the city we were placed in temporary housing until we would be

128

shipped to the north of South Korea. While there, I was assigned to the 107th Ordinance Maintenance Company. I had my choice of examining gun barrels of large cannons or heading up an automotive repair platoon. I chose the repair assignment as I didn't want to go anywhere near the front. Our large cannon batteries were taking fire from the enemy and occasionally one of our cannons would blow up.

As the leader of the auto repair platoon, I was called up one day to retrieve a vehicle right at the front line. They gave me a tank recovery vehicle that itself looked like a tank. I had to drive through our infantry lines, areas made up of many foxholes with our soldiers in them. When we reached the vehicle, we attached it to the tank and were ready for its recovery. Nearby soldiers warned me that, when I turned the engine on, the Chinese would probably lob mortar artillery on us since they used listening devices to detect enemy movements. When we did turn the engine on, a large cloud of smoke went up that showed them our position, but in spite of that no rounds came in on us and we went safely through our lines to our ordinance outfit.

There were no enemy attacks on my outfit while I was there from January of 1952 to June, 1953. But the war had virtually come to an end while I was still there, north of the 38th Parallel.

Once my outfit was bombed by our own Navy planes. Apparently, from reports we had read at the time, a Navy plane was damaged over North Korea and was returning to base when it either released its bombs intentionally or accidentally before landing. We weren't directly hit, but the bombs destroyed a unit next to us, and the headquarters building itself was gone. Korean money from a strong box came floating down in the air.

Some shrapnel dropped down on me, but I wasn't wounded. Our big job was to help the bombed unit get the injured to a hospital.

My unit was erroneously positioned in a flat area that turned out to be a river bed. When the monsoon season started and the river rose, it was the duty of the guard to inform the Captain if anything unusual happened. But the guard watched the river rise six to eight feet without informing him. As a result, when we all woke up the next morning, the water was completely surrounding us. We were on an island. We tried to cross the river in our biggest ammo truck, but were washed down in the rapidly moving water. The drivers abandoned the truck to avoid being submerged.

Since it was obvious that no trucks could navigate the river, we rigged a breaches-buoy (a term used by the Navy) to get mail and people off the island. When the river subsided, once again we could continue our mission.

As we were pondering our new circumstances, a helicopter came out of the sky and landed. An Army colonel disembarked and offered help to our officer in charge. He was told that we needed fresh water. To that, the colonel retorted, "What are you talking about? You're surrounded by water. Boil it!" Then he flew away.

The side effect of the monsoon storm was that our complete shower unit swept down the river. This was disappointing to me because I had built it. It had been very effective at heating water but made an enormous roar when operating. Our soldiers had wanted such a unit, so I had designed and built an eight-unit one for them. I had used water from the river and an old Jeep engine to drive a used pump. Water was heated in steel cans with blowtorches and diesel fuel. The shower was a raging success until the monsoon came, but I had to warn everybody who used it that the water was too polluted to drink.

The shower wasn't all I built. Later there was also an amphitheater, a stage, and a dressing room to house the USO girls that were to come. The whole thing worked well and we had a number of USO shows there. My biggest problem was keeping officers and enlisted men from being too friendly with the girls.

While I was there, one of the warrant officers received a poor grade for his performance, which meant that he would not be promoted. He had thirty years in the service and that mark would mean the end of his career. He told us that he was going to shoot our commanding officer. My friend and I decided to try to disarm him, plying him with drinks while telling him how ridiculous shooting the man would be. In time we were able to get his 45-automatic pistol away from him. He finally went to sleep and by the next day his anger was gone. We may have saved his life because that CO had two pistols at his bedside ready to fire. He also had a carbine with a bayonet in case the Chinese came over the hill.

Rumor had it that this CO was the oldest reserve officer serving in Korea. He had a very loose way of commanding, almost to the point of disregard for the role he was supposed to play. It was disappointing to me to see that this same CO would sometimes gather up some of the battalion officers and disappear into Seoul for two to four days for "recreation." When he got back, it was my job to resurrect his jeep into a vehicle workable for the next trip. It had gone over 50 miles of rough road, rice paddies filled with rocks. Occasionally there was a hole there big enough for jeeps to fall into.

One day I was called up to the headquarters tent and informed that my brother, a Captain in the U. S. Army Engineers, was there. As he was walking toward me across a field I wondered who this sloppy-looking person was. I finally recognized Steve, on the road through North Korea for a number of days, inspecting roads and bridges. We celebrated his visit by consuming a fifth of Johnny Walker before he left.

Sometimes we took some recreation which included hunting pheasants that the South Koreans told us were everywhere. (We didn't find any.) We didn't step on any of the mines, but on those days we even walked in some of the mined areas. That was really unwise. The nearby river was clear, even if it was polluted, and we swam in it, amusing ourselves by retrieving bullets fired into the water from a 45-automatic pistol. I dived into the water and waited. At first the bullets my friends shot into the air went very rapidly--about 900 feet per second--but by the time I caught them underwater they had slowed to almost no velocity.

I had left the country as a first lieutenant in the Ordinance Corps. I was also the labor officer. All duties in the company were distributed among the officers, so each wore many hats. Being the labor officer was interesting because I had to be sure that each Korean mechanic was completely provided for. We took each of them into Seoul every Friday so they could be with their families during the weekend. On payday I paid each of them in the currency of their country, which amounted to a large number of bills, half a cubic foot of currency!

I made many friends among the South Koreans and felt that they were good people. They certainly helped the war effort. Over all, my time in their country was quite a growing experience for me. It did a lot for my maturity.

SALT MINE HAUNTS

Keith Bardin

It must have been the spring of '67, or thereabouts, and certainly the day before the Easter holiday. Now a salt mine may seem a strange place for two Columbia University physics post-docs and a graduate student to be working, but we had felt it preferable to the coal mine we had looked at. Coal mines are definitely dirty, while salt mines are just salty, and we needed one or the other.

We had spent over three years at the university inventing, developing, building, and finally testing apparatus for a major experiment, and the last major condition we needed was protection from cosmic rays--hence the salt mine, an operating mine of the Morton Salt Company, 1,900 feet under Lake Erie, part of the little town of Fairport, Ohio, a bit east of Cleveland. And yes, I mean "under."

At the time of which I write, we had finished setting up and were well along in accumulating data. It was an impressive layout. Since salt mines sometimes rain salty water inside, we had a little corrugated iron house for protection. Inside were three racks full of electronics and the "beast," a ton or so of cylindrical magnet with a kind of sunburst of detectors sticking out from its middle, a tutu on our iron hippopotamus, all artistically draped with interconnecting cables. The whole thing could easily have come out of some grade B sci-fi movie. It even made random "click-whirr" noises as our counts came in. *Our* blinking lights meant something, however.

Outside our little domain was the entrance gallery of the mine, and "gallery" is definitely the right word here. The ceiling was some 20 or 25 feet up, and the floor space must have been 30 feet by more than 100 feet, all brightly lit. Toward one end, not far from our house, was the main crew elevator, and, in a somewhat broader space in the gallery, the main ventilating blower for the entire mine, all five miles of it extending on under the lake.

This blower looked somewhat like a grossly oversized jet engine, with a 100-horsepower or so electric motor driving it, and a grossly oversized voice. It howled unremittingly, 24 hours every day, and took a good deal of getting used to, even inside our little house.

I was alone in the house that Friday afternoon before Easter, working on something. What it was I don't remember except that it must have been absorbing. Everything was working properly; there were no emergencies to handle, and things in the house were as placid as they ever got in the presence of the ventilating blower. Gradually, however, it began to dawn on me that it was a little *too* placid. I hadn't been hearing the usual noises of mine personnel going up and down the crew elevator! I took a quick look at my watch... Oops! Seven o'clock!

So I packed up my bag, put on my hard hat, trotted over to the elevator, and pushed the button. I waited... Nothing! The elevator power was off, which most probably meant everyone had gone home for the weekend. Except...there had to be guards in the topside guard shack, usually two of them, with a *telephone immediately in front of them!*

Aha! Immediate plan of action: go on into the mine where I knew there was a mine-level office with a telephone. Find a mine telephone book and phone the guards!

OK! I walked over to the door leading into the mine, which was a steel plate about five feet wide by seven feet tall, with a little square sliding door in it about face high. Pushing on the door wouldn't work; the air pressure on the door was too high. So I opened the little slide port, releasing a blast of wind that neatly took my hard hat off. Then I could open the big door. Picking up my hat, I closed the door and the port behind me. I walked 20 feet further down the passage, where I came to another door of the same ilk. It opened the same way, so after picking up my hat again, and closing the door and port the way I did before, I could continue into the mine to the office. That looked promising. There were several desks and a telephone. I just needed a phone book...

There was nothing on the desktops. I tried the desk drawers. Again nothing. Under desks? In odd corners? Still nothing. There were two or three odd phone numbers, without names, graffiti on the bare sheetrock, all of them full seven-digit numbers. That was no good. The mine system had just four-digit extensions. Things began to look serious...

Well, four digits means only 10,000 numbers......*only?* But what else *was* there to do? I thought that I would probably make it out before Monday. All right, I'd see how it went. (At least, I wouldn't have to wait long for an answer, with the phone right in front of the guard that way.) So, with just two rings per trial... Dial...*ring...ring...*click...new number...dial...*ring...ring...*

Fortunately, it became obvious very quickly that there were large blocks of numbers that just weren't connected, so I was able to eliminate them, greatly shortening the task. It actually wasn't much more than 20 minutes before I got...new number...dial...*ring...*"*Hello!*"...and was able to explain to the guard who and where I was. His response was interesting: "Oh, *you're* the one. We thought the place was spooked!" What had been happening, from the viewpoint of the very extensive processing plant above ground, was that a phone would ring in some odd corner of the plant, and a guard would start off after it only to have it cut off short. Then a new phone in an entirely different direction would start ringing, and on, and on, and *on*, for the whole 20 minutes I was dialing. I was giving them some exercise!

(Of course, in hindsight what I *should* have done was to let one of the first phones I reached just go on ringing for five minutes or so, giving a guard time to reach it. However, that was far too rational for my state of mind at the time. Besides, I had no idea how many of those numbers would just ring inside locked offices.)

All well and good. I had made contact but I was still down in that hole. So, I asked, "Could someone please turn on the elevator so I can get out?" Well, there was a hang-up: the guards told me that they couldn't do that. It took the mine supervisor. Fortunately, he lived close by and they could call him. So I sat by the phone and waited, wondering if I had to wait for this fellow to finish his dinner before he showed up. I was getting rather hungry myself.

Actually, it didn't take very long before the phone in front of me rang, with the supervisor on the other end. He was very helpful but only in his own way. For reasons that presumably were clear to him but were certainly not evident to me, he asked me to come up, not in the crew elevator with which I was familiar, but in the salt elevator, a very different affair. My adventures, it seemed, were not yet over!

The salt elevator car was about the shape and size of one of those railroad bulk carrier cars, turned on end. The bottom end, which was hidden in the lower end of the shaft, presumably had some kind of a dump door, while the top was open above and on one side except for a really coarse grid across the car just below the edge of the open side. That grid was there to limit the size of the salt chunks that were loaded into the car to relatively small boulders, boulders that seemed to me alarmingly close to the size of my boots, considering that I had to stand there on the grid, with perhaps 30 feet of empty car yawning under my feet!

I knew the drill for using that elevator, having seen workers go casually up and down that way. I had to get onto the grid and then reach out and around a little corner to give a coded series of tugs to a signal rope: "Hoist away, man aboard." A different signal was used for a load of salt, suggesting to me that the power used for a load of salt might mash me through the grid. So I carefully arranged my feet on the grid and gave the signal. The car took off like a startled jackrabbit, *much* faster than I expected, and I felt that I was fortunate that my knees hadn't buckled.

It was an impressively fast 1,900-foot trip, and when I got to the top and saw the winch that was used, I was impressed all over again. The drum that cable was wrapped around must have been twelve feet in diameter or more, around one end of which was the biggest bull gear I had ever seen. Starting that beast up must have dimmed lights all over town.

So ended my adventure. No one will be surprised to learn that, thereafter, all three of us kept a more careful eye on the time when working in our little house. After all, we still didn't know the phone extension for the guard shack.

NOTES ON THE CONTRIBUTORS

Keith Bardin is a retired physicist and electronic engineer with extensive aerospace experience. He has strong interests in classical music and digital photography and is an author only on those rare occasions when his erratic muse passes through town.

Norman Gould, a physician, considers himself a lucky man because he married a wonderful woman.

Richard Gousha served 25 years as Superintendent of Schools in Ohio, Wisconsin, and Delaware. Among other leadership positions, he became a professor in the Graduate School faculty and Dean of the School of Education at Indiana University, Bloomington.

Barnet Greene is a hard worker, a blunt talker, and a person who believes in integrity and civility. He accepts life as it is and has a wife who finds him both kind and thoughtful.

Larry Hawkinson is a retired mathematics teacher and department head (Gunn High, Palo Alto), as well as a retired commander in the United States Naval Reserve.

William Johnson and his wife, Bobbie, applied deeply held religious beliefs to the medical services which they provided throughout the needy world.

Dorothy Horning is a Saratoga Retirement Community resident with a lifetime of wonderful memories and making more every day.

Thomas McCollough is a business man from Columbus, Ohio. He had careers in both the private and public sectors. The selections in this book are from his memoirs.

Bill Murphy and his wife, Jean, celebrated their 48th wedding anniversary in 2008 with their six children and their families. The incredible journey that began in Paris many years ago promises to bring ever-increasing moments of joy and fulfillment.

Alan Purchase is thankful for the timing of his birth with the Air Force training program which resulted in his being in combat for only the last six months of the Second World War.

Janet Rafferty's life has taken her from small-town Midwest to the heart of Manhattan's fashion district and back across the country to the Bay Area of California.

Malcolm E. (Buck) Sample was a Special Agent in the FBI for 30 years, the Corporate Security Manager for National Semiconductor Corporation, and then formed his own multinational consulting company.

Elizabeth Léonie Simpson, developmental psychologist, has written fiction, nonfiction, and poetry throughout her life span.

Carl Szybalski is continuing to teach his 12-year-old grandson the basketball game he loves. Sports, politics, and music have always been important to this grandfather.

Deanna Viale's life has been challenged by polio and enriched by her teaching experience with first and second graders.

Elsworth Welch and his wife, Jackie, have lived in Saratoga, California since 1949. He taught chemistry at Los Gatos High School for 37 years.

Irving Yabroff completed a Ph. D. in Electrical Engineering at Stanford University. After ending 26 years at the Stanford Research Institute, he founded a software company in Los Gatos.